THE LORD'S SUPPER

A Biblical Interpretation

by
SCOTT McCORMICK, Jr.

THE WESTMINSTER PRESS
Philadelphia

LIBRARY OF CONGRESS CATALOG CARD No. 66-10161

PUBLISHED BY THE WESTMINSTER PRESS ®
PHILADELPHIA, PENNSYLVANIA
PRINTED IN THE UNITED STATES OF AMERICA

To My Teacher
BALMER HANCOCK KELLY
with appreciation and esteem

CONTENTS

INTRODUCTION

"This is my body. . . . This is my blood" — familiar words in the church's worship, attended by equally familiar actions. But what does it all mean? Better, what should it mean? This study was initially prompted by an inability to correlate confessional statements with the Bible. The statements seemed to hold more mystery than was called for and less meaning than might be expected. An ordained minister, I nonetheless felt like an initiate to a secret society — one who knows the password well enough but is hazy about what is going on in the meeting. So the study was begun. Soon it became obvious that I would have to lay ecclesiastical pronouncements aside and deal exclusively with the Biblical teaching.

Evidently I had not been alone in my confusion. Discussions with fellow clergymen across denominational lines have frequently revealed a rather widespread dissatisfaction in the matter. Not that I have been talking only with heretics! There just seems to be a lack of precision in traditional explanations that relate eucharistic practice to New Testament teaching. Most are agreed that the Lord's Supper is an extremely important juncture in Christian worship. And all admit that sensitive souls, in the eucharistic setting alone, find it a "meaningful" experience. But meaningful in what sense? Is it to be mainly a subjective thing, more or less at the mercy of aesthetics and the state of one's digestion? Or is there a meaning it

ought to have for all, a meaning specifically derived from New
Testament terminology and thought? If so, can our explanations
of that meaning be given authority by first appealing, not to
ambiguous or controversial ecclesiastical definitions, but to
the Biblical witness itself? Protestantism, especially in its grow-
ing ecumenical concern, must make the endeavor.

The pundits have long been wrestling with this, and their
labors have yielded excellent studies. Generally, however, the
best works either have been beyond the parish minister's habit
or have been concerned with only certain aspects of the New
Testament teaching, not with the Biblical material as a whole.
Our current revival in liturgics notwithstanding, the fruits of
serious scholarship have yet to make their way to the Communion table via the local pastor's study. So this little book
is written for ministers and theological students who feel a
need for more clarity and Biblical relevance in interpreting the
Sacrament.

Now a word about procedure. It is reasonably clear that we
must go back to the Last Supper itself for what Jesus meant in
"instituting" the Sacrament. For instance, when the Corinthians fell into eucharistic malpractice, Paul pointed them to
Jesus' last meal as the corrective (I Cor. 11:23-25). The
Synoptic writers likewise reveal a fundamental agreement between the Last Supper and the Lord's Supper. Notably Mark's
account of Jesus' eucharistic words (Mark 14:22-24) betrays
a liturgical formula that was most certainly in very early use.
That is to say, a formula of worship subsequent to the event
of the Supper was used in good conscience to report the event
itself. The Last Supper and early eucharistic practice were
therefore assumed to bear essentially the same meaning. And
although many have doubted that Jesus actually originated the
Synoptic and Pauline sacramental teaching, the validity of his
authorship of it now seems secure. (Cf. Appendix C.) Hence,
to know what the Lord's Supper should mean for us, we must
enter the upper room.

Yet as one enters there, one observes that it is a thoroughly

Jewish room. To even an occasional student of the Old Testament, the atmosphere of Hebraic thought and theology is readily apparent. Here is a Jew, said to be the Messiah, celebrating the Passover with his disciples, whose initial number, twelve, foretells the new Israel, the Messiah's community. (Cf. Appendix D.) He speaks of his approaching death in the language of sacrifice and gives it significance in terms of the covenant. He refers to his fulfillment of the atoning, covenantal mission of Second Isaiah's " Servant," and he points to the feasting to come in the Kingdom of God. Such references are not to be slighted. From them it is evident that no adequate understanding of the Supper can be gained apart from its Old Testament background. Failure to consider it so, as if Jesus and the gospel came out of a vacuum, basically accounts for most confusion about the Sacrament. Worse still is to suppose that it reflects twentieth-century thinking! More exactly, therefore, the object of this study is an interpretation of the eucharistic words and actions with special attention to their Old Testament or Hebraic foundations.

So this is not a devotional book or a series of suggestions for liturgical practice, but an exercise in Biblical theology, attempting to look at Jesus' eucharistic teaching within the framework of Israel's faith as the New Testament accounts themselves direct us. Its scope has required that certain major critical questions be treated in an appendix, and then only summarily; but one hopes the discussion and notations there will give starting directions for anyone wanting to pursue the questions himself.

An even greater hope is that some may be led, by way of old Israel, to a fuller understanding of the Supper of Him who came out of Israel to redeem us and who sits at table with us.

I THE PERSON AND GIFT OF JESUS' SACRIFICE

In their simplest form, the bread and wine sayings of eucharistic observance hold up before us the person and gift of Jesus' sacrifice — what it meant for him and what it means for us. For him it meant utter obedience; for us it means God's free gift of salvation. This is precisely and primarily what confronts us in the Sacrament: the saving offer of that Lamb of God who is Sacrifice in Person.

The New Testament is a book about sacrifice. Its foremost concern is the significance of Jesus' sacrificial, atoning work. The issue was not otherwise at the Last Supper. The question of this chapter is how Jesus' sacrifice is depicted sacramentally, according to the particular words: "This is my body. . . . This is my blood. . . ." Only eight words; yet the fundamental significance of the cross, both personally for the Savior and redemptively for us, is implied in these abbreviated sayings.

We must look at each of the words in detail and in the parallel form in which they are cast, asking all the time what import they would have for Hebrews. To do so is to recapture the vital mood of the upper room and the vitality of eucharistic worship, meeting nothing less than God's gift of salvation that issues from the sacrifice of Jesus' person.

But first let us get our bearings. The Synoptic and Pauline accounts of the Supper do not report everything that was said and done between the breaking of the bread and the singing of the closing hymn. Nor do we have even a summary report formulated immediately thereafter, as might be contained in the minutes of a committee meeting. Instead, the descriptions of the proceedings are written out of postresurrection faith, which is also the position of the earliest ascertainable traditions behind the reports. Therefore, if one asks how much the disciples understood of the Supper's meaning while it was being held, a precise answer is out of reach. We can only say that they did not comprehend it then as clearly and completely as they later did — a fact that the Gospels stress about the disciples' preresurrection understanding of Jesus' words and actions in general.[1] Acts One and Two of a play make more sense when Act Three is finished and the play is ended.

Rather, the question to ask concerns the meaning attributed to the Last Supper as it was viewed from the cross-resurrection vantage point. The accounts of the Supper are at the same time historical and interpretative. Accordingly, what they indicate of Jesus' sacrifice should not be isolated from what the early church said about it elsewhere. The eucharistic words are a part of New Testament theology, not a departure from it.

THE SACRIFICIAL FRAMEWORK OF THE SUPPER

Even before Jesus spoke of his death in terms of the sacramental bread and wine, the stage had been set for a sacrificial motif. This is evident at once in the Passion Week tradition. The accounts of that week, for all their seemingly easy narration of events, are shot through with sacrificial overtones. Jesus has come to Jerusalem as one whose business was to shoulder

---

[1] Questions must have been raised. Peter objected to the foot washing (John 13:8), and Jesus' eucharistic words could hardly have met with silence! Significantly, Passover ritual prescribed a place for the proceedings to be explained. After the resurrection, when the disciples finally saw that Jesus' eucharistic reference to his death did not spell nonsense and defeat, they could recall the explanation of that which initially they could not fully grasp. Also, in his postresurrection meetings with them, he likely discussed the matter still further.

the iniquity of us all (Isa. 53:6). He entered the city on a beast of burden, fulfilling the Messianic prophecy of Zech. 9:9, and then straightway went into the Temple, where he simply "looked round at everything" (Mark 11:11).[2] This was a twofold action designed to announce that he is the Messiah who is personally identified with the place where Israel's sacrifices were slaughtered.[3] His identification with the Temple is subsequently maintained in his entering it daily to teach (Luke 19:47; 21:37-38). As a whole it serves to say that Jesus is not Messiah only but is Messiah *and* Suffering Servant: he is Messiah who is Sacrifice!

Also, the occasion of the Last Supper was a sacrificial meal, the Passover of the Jews.[4] Quite aside from the eucharistic words, therefore, the thoughts of Jesus and the Twelve were already moving in a sacrificial context.

THE PERSON OF SACRIFICE

In considering now the bread and wine sayings as they relate to the Person of sacrifice, we need to recognize them as complementary. The sayings are finally to be taken together, and not each by itself. They so appear in all four accounts of the Supper,[5] one saying following on the heels of the other, even though the meal proper originally came between them (Luke 22:20; I Cor. 11:25). The two were understood as belonging together, so that Mark (ch. 14:22-24) and Matthew

[2] Scripture quotations, other than mine, are from the Revised Standard Version of the Bible. *Italics in such quotations are always mine.*

[3] In stressing this, Mark (ch. 11:15-17) reserves the Temple cleansing for Jesus' second appearance there.

[4] Whereas the Synoptists identify the Last Supper as a Passover and date it Nisan 15, the date for Passover observance, Johannine tradition dates it at least twenty-four hours earlier. The problem is surveyed in Appendix D, where I take the position that although the Johannine dating is to be preferred as that of the official calendar, incidental evidence from both the Synoptic and Johannine accounts of Passion Week attests to the paschal character of the meal itself.

[5] The shorter reading of Luke's account, omitting the wine saying in ch. 22:19b-20, is inferior; see Appendix A.

(ch. 26:26-28) record them as if nothing at all had separated them.

This " togetherness " of the sayings is confirmed in the work of recent critics who, endeavoring to uncover the oldest form of the eucharistic words, suggest that the earliest text read thus:

Take; this is my body.
This is my blood of the covenant which is poured out for the sake of many.

This reconstructed text is significantly identical with the words of interpretation as recorded in Mark. And Mark's account, since it has numerous Semitisms and Palestinian idioms, is judged to represent an extremely early tradition.[6] The " togetherness " of the bread and wine sayings is therefore attested way back in the church's appreciation of their meaning. So both the literary and historical evidence dictate that the sayings are to be regarded as complementary.

Jesus' self-reference in terms of his " body." As for Jesus' intent in the bread saying, primary attention must be given the word *sōma*, translated " body." What did he mean in speaking of his *body?* He meant his entire person as sacrificed, not just the substance of his flesh.

Although scholars have differed on the exact Aramaic word spoken — whether *guphi* or *bisri* — the reference was certainly all-inclusive. In case of *guphi*, the emphasis would be " I myself "; in case of *bisri*, it would be on the sacrificial aspect of the reference. But both emphases, the personal and the sacrificial, were no doubt present, whichever word was used. *Guphi*, focusing on Jesus' person, would do so with a view to his being sacrificed, since the saying about his " body " was accompanied by that about his blood. *Bisri*, on the other hand, would have been taken to signify the whole person in sacrifice, not merely the flesh substance.

This all-inclusive, personal reference of " body " must ulti-

[6] Joachim Jeremias, *The Eucharistic Words of Jesus*, tr. by Arnold Ehrhardt (The Macmillan Company, 1955), pp. 106–132.

mately be understood from what the Hebrew believed about individual personality. And here as much as anywhere else the modern mind runs into a radically foreign notion. It requires of us some serious adjustments in thought.

Our trouble at this point is that we have been conditioned by Greek thinking more than we are likely aware. A basic distinction is supposed to exist between body and soul or flesh and spirit. These may be deemed interrelated, each being influenced by the other; still, moderns are wont to regard them basically as separate entities. The individual is thus a conglomeration of heterogeneous parts: part flesh, part soul, and/or part spirit, with the body holding these together until death. Then the soul flees its earthly abode to live on as a disembodied spirit. This Greek idea, enhancing the "immortal" soul as naturally different from the corruptible body or flesh, is widely proclaimed today, even by seminary graduates who ought to know better. And preachers have been getting away with the idea, to almost everyone's delight. After all, it is a comfort for countless people.

But it is not Biblical! In the Hebrew view, a man is no more part flesh and part soul or spirit than he is part "snips and snails and puppy dogs' tails." What we differentiate as the "psychical" and "physical" in man were considered to be virtually one and the same. If the Hebrew were to use such terms, he would define the individual to be a "psychophysical" being.[7]

This concept of man's essential oneness, which governs our interpretation of "body" in the bread saying, is particularly revealed in the Old Testament usage of *nephesh* (soul), *rûah* (spirit), and *bâsar* (flesh). These terms may refer either to the life principle or to that which makes a man what he is; or, more importantly here, they may denote his person or self, his

[7] The term "psychophysical," implying a consolidation of what is essentially psychical and what is essentially physical, suggests a distinction the Hebrew did not think to make. But it is used to express the Hebrew concept in modern speech.

total being. For instance, it is said that "the LORD God formed
man of dust from the ground, and breathed into his nostrils the
breath of life; and man became a living *nephesh*" (Gen. 2:7).
Not man was *given* a *nephesh* or soul, but man *became* a soul
— flesh, blood, bones, and all! That is what man *is*, not *has*.
One's *nephesh*, therefore, was not regarded as something that
flies from his body at death and thereby extends his individual
existence. To the contrary, at death a man is a dead *nephesh*, a
corpse (cf. Num. 6:6; 19:11, 13; Lev. 21:11). Hence, *nephesh*
with a suffix could stand for the personal pronoun: "Many
are saying of my *nephesh*, there is no help for him in God"
(Ps. 3:2).

Closely akin to *nephesh* but not always in exact parallel,
rûaḥ (spirit) connoted on a higher plane the purposeful life
of the individual, especially as he could be stimulated to various kinds of behavior or feeling. Originally the word signified
a wind or breath of air, hence a variable energy. As *rûaḥ*, man
himself is variable, particularly when activated by the *rûaḥ*
of the Lord. Physical prowess, prophetic ecstasy, mental dis-
ability, rare understanding, acute reverence toward God — all
such phenomena could be so explained.[8] When applied specifically to man, *rûaḥ* meant either the life principle [9] — God's
creatures die when he gathers their *rûaḥ* (Ps. 104:29); or it
denoted man's self-awareness: "Be not quick in thy *rûaḥ* to
anger" (Eccl. 7:9). So *nephesh* and *rûaḥ*, usually translated
"soul" and "spirit," speak not of entities fundamentally distinct from the body or flesh but instead have the whole man in
mind. To quote H. Wheeler Robinson, "The Hebrew idea of
personality is an animated body, and not an incarnated soul." [10]

[8] Cf. Judg. 14:6, 19; 15:14; I Sam. 10:6, 10; 16:15; Isa. 11:2-3. This
was not a "low" or psychologically naïve doctrine of man but a "high"
doctrine of God, who was believed to be personally and directly involved
in all the affairs of human life. Yet the doctrine did not, in Hebrew
thought, fall into the one-sided error of an ultra-Calvinistic or philo-
sophical determinism.

[9] So also *nephesh;* e.g., II Kings 1:13.

[10] H. Wheeler Robinson, "Hebrew Psychology," *The People and the
Book*, ed. by Arthur S. Peake (Oxford: The Clarendon Press, 1925),

The usage of *bâsar* (flesh) only strengthens this feeling for totality. Occasionally it simply means man; for example, " My mouth will speak the praise of the LORD, and let all *bâsar* bless his holy name for ever and ever " (Ps. 145:21). At other times it signifies man under judgment, as in prophetic words that God will judge " all flesh " (cf. Isa. 66:16; Jer. 25:31;45:5). Elsewhere it is in parallel with *nephesh*, standing for the personal pronoun: " my *nephesh* thirsts for thee; my *bâsar* faints for thee " (Ps. 63:1). More precisely, *bâsar* may denote man contrasted with God: " All flesh is grass " — withering grass! — " but the word of our God will stand for ever " (Isa. 40:6-8). Man as *bâsar* is but " a wind that passes and comes not again " (Ps. 78:39). Whereas God is almighty and everlasting, *bâsar* is weak (II Chron. 32:8) and bound to die (Gen. 6:3). This is all to say that man does not *have* flesh, he *is* flesh: the whole of him is flesh.

When *nephesh*, *rûah*, and *bâsar* are used of the individual, it is therefore the whole man in view. Each term merely considers him from a different perspective. As *nephesh* he is man as a conscious being whose life is rooted in the life given and controlled by God. As *rûah* he is all that plus one who is especially susceptible to the influential, energizing *rûah* of the Lord. As *bâsar* he is again the whole man, but regarded in his external existence and thus, as weak *bâsar*, contrasted with God, who is all-powerful *Rûah*. The distinctions in these terms are finally to be seen as relational rather than essential.

An analogy is found in the different terms we apply to ourselves. A man reading this page may be a husband and a father as well as a son. Each term considers him from a different angle, in view of a definite relationship. But surely we do not mean to say that the man is only part son! only part husband! only part father!

It is this conception of human personality which accounts for the fact that late Jewish belief in conscious life after death

---

p. 362. Much of what I say about *nephesh*, *rûah*, and *bâsar* is a summation of his discussion.

took the form of a resurrection body. The Hebrew simply could not conceive of such a life without a body, a disembodied spirit or soul flitting about somewhere in the universe. And it is this which explains the New Testament's relentless concern with Jesus' being bodily raised from death and the meaning of that for faith. "If Christ has not been raised," then the Christian schooled in Hebraic thought can only conclude that "faith is futile" and "those . . . who have fallen asleep in Christ have perished" and "we are of all men most to be pitied" (I Cor. 15:17-19)! Whether in the upper room, speaking of himself sacramentally, or lying in Joseph's tomb, Christ *is* a body. It is the New Testament's austere realism.

But to counter this view, someone will ask what Paul meant when he confided to friends that he would just as soon die right then, "depart and be with Christ" (Phil. 1:23). The apostle seems to be saying that immediately upon death the believer is ushered into Christ's presence — and many a man today wants to think it about a loved one who has passed beyond the shadows. But did Paul mean to imply that he would then live without any kind of body? Not at all! For, as we shall see, he believed that the Christian is really united with Christ, is a member of Christ's own body, and is already sharing Christ's resurrected life. If there is a conscious existence for the Christian during the interim between his earthly demise and a future resurrection of the dead, it is most assuredly not a disembodied existence. It is, rather, existence in the body of Christ, already raised by God and alive.

Now, as a Hebrew, Jesus doubtlessly shared this view of human personality, considering the individual as a psychophysical being. Contradictory evidence would come as a shock, and there is no sufficient reason to believe that he did not share it. In sacramentally referring to his "body" as sacrificed, he was therefore referring to *himself* as sacrificed.

But could the church expect *sōma* in Greek accounts of the eucharistic words to be thus understood? Apparently, for elsewhere in the New Testament *sōma* often refers to the whole person or self.[11] It appears in the records of Jesus' teaching about one's "body" being full of light or darkness, where the reference is obviously to one's person or being (Matt. 6:22-23; Luke 11:34, 36). It is met again in Paul's statement that "our old self was crucified with him so that the sinful body" — i.e., the whole sinful personality — "might be destroyed, and we might no longer be enslaved to sin" (Rom. 6:6). An even clearer use is in the exhortation, "Present your bodies as a living sacrifice" (Rom. 12:1); in other words, "Present *yourselves*." One is also reminded of the apostle's warning against illicit sexual relations: "Do you not know that he who joins himself to a prostitute becomes one *sōma* with her? For, as it is written, 'The two shall become one *sarx*'" (I Cor. 6:16). Such a parallel usage of "body" and "flesh" would be clumsy had Paul been speaking as a classical Greek. Yet it is quite natural for a Hebrew, who would make no essential distinctions between one's body and the substance of it or between one's body and person. Likewise, "husbands should love their wives as their own *bodies*. He who loves his wife loves *himself*." (Eph. 5:28.) Here again, with *sōma* and *heautou* in parallel, "body" denotes the whole person.

The striking thing to note especially of Paul's use of "body" in this sense is that he was writing mainly to non-Jews, yet was assuming on their part a certain appreciation of Hebrew psychology. This apostle to the Gentiles evidently had instructed his charges in Hebraic thought. How much more Hebrew thinking must have prevailed in the Jerusalem church, whose members were Jews! And it was from that church that the tradition of Jesus' eucharistic words emanated. Significantly, the oneness of the individual is maintained throughout the New Testament, with no essential distinction necessarily made between one's body and one's person or self.[12] The reference of

[11] A precedent had been established in the Septuagint (cf. LXX Gen. 34:29; 36:6; 47:12; I Chron. 28:1).

[12] An exception might seem to be the Matthean version of Jesus' saying about not fearing "those who kill the body but cannot kill the soul" (ch. 10:28; cf. Luke 12:4, omitting the contrast). But note that the saying

"body" in the bread saying can therefore only be taken to reflect the Hebrew psychology. It denotes the sacrifice of Jesus with respect to his entire person.

The church's discernment of what the atonement involved substantiates this interpretation of "body." According to the New Testament, Jesus' sacrifice was not simply a slaughter, the slaying of a victim unaware of or opposed to its fate. The offering by which men are redeemed involved for Jesus a knowledge of God's will, arrived at through faith, and a voluntary submission thereto. It involved his obedience; it involved his whole person; it involved *him!* His was a total, not a partial, sacrifice. And it is that sacrifice, the sacrifice of a Person, to which the Lord's Supper calls attention.

Jesus' reference to his obedience unto death. Now the necessity that Jesus' sacrifice involve his obedience is indicated in the particular condition of the sacramental elements. The bread, relating to his "body," is *broken* bread. This is to say, interpreting "body" as above, that he referred to *himself* as broken. And how was Jesus himself broken? In his utter submission to God, as, for analogy, an animal is "broken" in being brought under the control of its master. The *will* is broken in such cases. The animal, of course, does not lose its will, but learns to do its master's will instead. So was Jesus broken, according to the bread saying. His ego or self, his very person, was broken under God's mastery of him.

Once again, this is exactly what the Gospels show us of

is in an eschatological context: though death will come to men for Jesus' sake, those enduring to the end will be saved (Matt. 10:21-22). Hence, the contrast in v. 28 between body and soul is not necessarily essential but, instead, may simply be viewing the whole person from different perspectives: "body" referring to the person naturally subject to death, "soul" referring to the same person who can receive eternal life in Christ via resurrection. The saying in Matthew (as the Lucan version) then takes on kerygmatic force: "Do not fear those who can kill you but cannot remove you from the victory of God's kingdom in me!" Jesus is reported to have said the same of himself: "Destroy this temple, and in three days I will raise it up" (John 2:19). He was speaking, says John (v. 21), "of the temple of his body"!

Jesus. In the narrow sense of the word, his *body* was not broken (John 19:32-33) — but *he* was! He was broken in surrender, broken in the sense of a complete denial of self, yielding unreservedly to him whose will took precedence over everything else. To read through the accounts of Jesus' ministry is to gasp at the sight unfolding there. From the temptation experience in the wilderness to the agony of Gethsemane, it unfolds with intensifying horror. It is the sight of a Man who is like all other men and yet who, at immeasurable personal cost, is not; the sight of a man who knows the tempter's power, only infinitely more than we do, because *he* never succumbs to get relief from it. He is a man inherently beset, as are we, by the weakness of the flesh. Still, he is hit again and again by his Master's exacting demands, till he has no will of his own remaining but to do his Father's will. Never before, nor ever since, was there a son made subject to this! No other son could take it. He confesses he would prefer that the cup of suffering be removed from him — nay, *prays* that it be removed — but he knows in God's purpose that it must not be; hence, " Nevertheless not my will, but thine, be done" (Luke 22:42). Already in Gethsemane, with the cross still ahead of him, every last ounce of secret reservation is sweating out of him "like great drops of blood falling down upon the ground" (v. 44). And we are reminded of his words earlier that night likening himself to the *broken* bread! This is the one man who is broken completely, broken in utter obedience.

The consequence of Jesus' obedience was death, which brings us to the condition of the sacramental wine. The wine that he related to his blood was outpoured wine, wine in a cup. We have observed that early liturgical practice indicates that the bread and wine sayings are complementary. Accordingly, the wine saying shows to what extent Jesus is understood as broken: namely, to the extent of outpoured blood. His sacrifice involved obedience *unto death;* together the bread and wine sayings stress the fact. The latter brings out the full implications of the former: Jesus is sacramentally depicted as

broken in his whole person, broken in obedience to the final
extremity of blood being spilled. "The sacramental unity,"
wrote P. T. Forsyth,

was a personal one. Christ did not say, " I give myself to you in two
half parts," in two instalments as it were — life and death. The gift
of Himself was completely symbolised in the broken food. The
wine does not add something new, but points the real inner meaning of the bread, as the Cross does the person.[13]

So we are reminded in the Sacrament that, for Jesus, the
central issue in his atoning work was obedience, and at that,
obedience in life as well as in death. Indeed, it was not so much
his obedience *in* death as *unto* death that constituted the perfect offering in our behalf. The reference to his outpoured
blood, preceded as it is by the reference to his broken body,
fixes our eyes on the cross to see it not merely as a lonely sta-
tion in Jesus' life but as the place where his sacrifice culmi-
nated. It was the place to which his obedience, the body-break-
ing process, took him.

The Gift Issuing from Jesus' Sacrifice

Recognizing that the eucharistic bread and wine refer to
Jesus' whole person in sacrificial obedience unto death, we now
observe that his sacrifice issues in a gift for men: that is, the
gift of salvation, *which we are offered in the Lord's Supper
itself*. The sacramental representation of this gift is primarily
seen in the eucharistic *actions*, to be discussed in the chapter
that follows. However, the idea of the gift is also implied in the
words of interpretation themselves, particularly two words relating to the elements: *touto* ("this") and *estin* (customarily
translated "is"). Each of these can easily be misread, yet both
are notoriously crucial to any interpretation of the Supper.

First, then, to what does *touto* refer in the sayings *"This* is
my body"* and *"This* is my blood"? Certainly not to the ac-

[13] P. T. Forsyth, *The Church and the Sacraments* (London: Independent
Press, Ltd., 1917), p. 252.

tions of breaking and pouring but to the elements themselves as being, or about to be, distributed. Mark's record of the bread saying, for one, does not read: "*I break;* this is my body." Rather, it reads: "*You take;* this is my body" (Mark 14:22). Similarly, "this" in the wine saying refers to wine in a cup: "This cup which is poured out for you" (Luke 22:20; cf. I Cor. 11:25). All four accounts of the eucharistic words relate them directly to the distribution of the elements, not to the fracturing of the one and the outpouring of the other. The bread is already broken, the wine already poured.

From this reference of *touto* we see that the mode of Jesus' sacrifice is no concern in the sacramental symbolism. It is not Jesus in the act of being broken to the extent of outpoured blood, but Jesus as *already* broken to that extent, who is portrayed here. His sacrificial obedience is depicted not as something in motion but as completed, finished. At the Last Supper the cross was thus sacramentally anticipated as a historical fact, a *fait accompli.* Jesus spoke of himself as dead, not as dying; as having done his obedience, not as doing it. Only in departure from the eucharistic words, therefore, may one view the Last Supper, and consequently the Lord's Supper, as something in which the sacrificing of Christ either occurs or recurs.[14] The words allude to that sacrificing as already having happened, not as going on then and there. The gift that the Sacrament holds for us is the product of a *completed* sacrifice.

And that leads us to the other word, *estin.* If *touto* refers to the broken bread and outpoured wine as being or about to be distributed, the significance of their distribution must be seen in regard to this word "is." In what sense *is* the bread Jesus' broken body or self, and the wine his outpoured blood? It is questionable that an Aramaic equivalent of *estin* would have been used in such a construction in Jesus' day. The Aramaic was likely, "This my body. . . . This my blood. . . ." But since the church inserted *estin* in Greek translations of the eucharistic formula, one had best consider this word in order

14 Cf. *infra,* pp. 74–75.

to get at the original meaning of the formula.

Three distinct interpretations are readily at hand. The first of these, reading *estin* substantively, would indicate the bread and wine to be Jesus' body and blood in actual substance. It is hardly justifiable, however, to suppose that the disciples thought they were drinking Jesus' blood, either in the upper room or at subsequent celebrations of the Sacrament. To Jews the consumption of blood was horrifying. The law absolutely forbade it, on the grounds that the life resides in the blood.[15] Indeed, of Israel's many dietary laws, the blood prohibition alone was reckoned as binding for all Christians, whether they be of Jewish or Gentile stock (Acts 15:20, 29). Further, the broken bread and outpoured wine could not have been at the Last Supper the actual substance of a completed sacrifice which at the moment was *un*completed. Equally telling is the fact that a substantive reading of *estin* is not possible in the wine saying as recorded by Paul and Luke: "This cup [which is poured out for you] is the new covenant in my blood" (I Cor. 11:25; Luke 22:20). Clearly, neither the cup nor its contents could actually *be* the new covenant! And it would be mere exegetical subjectivism to assume that *estin* should get one interpretation at one point and yet another elsewhere in varying forms of the eucharistic words.

A second interpretation, reading *estin* in a symbolical sense, would indicate that the bread and wine "stand for" or "represent" Jesus' body and blood. This interpretation is immediately relieved of certain difficulties of a purely substantive one. However, it is cumbered by entailing a symbolic consumption of blood. Are we at liberty to suppose that Jesus would have directed his disciples to do symbolically what they were prohibited to do in reality? Nor would a symbolic drinking of blood have been much less offensive to them than an actual drinking of it.[16] Also, it is difficult to see how, according to the

---

[15] Lev. 17:10-14; cf. chs. 3:17; 7:26-27; 19:26; Gen. 9:4; Deut. 12:16, 23-25; I Sam. 14:32-34.
[16] The eucharistic discourse of John 6:53-56, which does speak of a

Pauline and Lucan formulations, a cup of wine could be expected to symbolize a *covenant*, which is not an object but a relationship. And the clinching argument against this second interpretation of *estin* is the obvious superiority of the next one to be considered.

By far the least offensive interpretation of the eucharistic *estin* reads it not in a substantive or a merely symbolic sense but in a significative sense, viz., " This broken bread *means* my body. . . . This outpoured wine *means* my blood. . . ." It is the sense of the " to be " verb that we find in the introduction to a commentary on Jesus' parable of the soils: " Now the parable *is* this " (Luke 8:11). But what follows is manifestly *not* the parable; the parable itself is recorded previously, in vs. 5-8. Nor is what follows a representation of the parable. It is, rather, an interpretation of the parable's *meaning*. A precise translation of v. 11 would therefore read, " Now this is what the parable means. . . ." In this sense of *estin*, the bread and wine mean what Jesus himself means in his being broken to the extent of death — that is, salvation!

But there is more to commend it than simply its being the least offensive interpretation. The significance it attributes to the bread and wine not only would have been wholly unoffensive to Jews about to partake of the elements; it also implies for the Last Supper and the Lord's Supper a vitality native to Hebrew sacramentalism.

Although never strictly defined, sacramentalism flourished as an essential part of Judaism, in Jesus' time particularly.[17] Sacrifices, circumcision, rites of immersion, and other cere-

---

symbolic drinking of Jesus' blood, is a difficulty at this point. But its authenticity is questionable, and I doubt that the issue will ever be settled. There is no doubt, however, that consumption of blood was repulsive to the early Jewish Christians (Acts 15:20, 29), which is the fact to note here.

[17] Cf. Frank S. B. Gavin, *The Jewish Antecedents of the Christian Sacraments* (London: Society for Promoting Christian Knowledge, 1928), pp. 3–23, dealing with Old Testament data surviving into Rabbinic Judaism up to A.D. 200.

monials were considered effective means of mediating a
changed relationship between God and man. These were material means, to be sure, but that held no difficulty for the Hebrew. He would only have difficulty with our sacramental definitions today, which at best would strike him as weird. The
distinctions we make between "the inward and spiritual" and
"the outward and visible" suggest a basic duality in the
scheme of things. But Judaism in essence was radically non-
dualistic. No fundamental break was made between the spiritual and the physical. Everything in life was directly related to
God. So what we call sacramentalism — and are sometimes
embarrassed to explain or defend! — came naturally for the
Hebrew. Acts involving material means were easily regarded
as channels of various blessings. And as we shall see in Chapter II, divine gifts were often thought to be received specifically through eating and drinking!

This interpretation of *estin* implies such a vitality for the
Sacrament. Relating to the elements' distribution, it attributes
to them a redemptive significance. The bread and wine, in being offered to the worshiper, are charged with power. They
then mean the gift of salvation in Jesus' sacrificial person, the
gift to be imparted to men. Sacramentally speaking, this reading of *estin* is therefore Hebraic to the core. It bespeaks a vitality consistent with Israelite practice, whereas other readings
fly in the face of certain Hebrew beliefs and/or require an in-
consistent interpretation of *estin* for varying forms of the
eucharistic words.

Accordingly, what is contained in the sacramental bread and
wine is not the substance or symbol of Jesus' body and blood,
but the saving gift issuing from his sacrifice. The already
broken bread *means* his broken body-self, the already outpoured wine *means* his outpoured blood. Together they signify what *he* means in the obedient sacrifice of his entire person to the point of death. And what means Jesus in that sense?
Nothing less than God's salvation for men! And that, we know,
comes to them as a gift.

Hence, the bread and wine are not on the table merely to be viewed in mystic contemplation. They are there to be distributed, to be freely given and freely received. So we turn next to the sacramental reception of the gift, particularly in terms of the eucharistic actions.

II THE RECEPTION OF THE GIFT

A frequent error in eucharistic practice has been to slight the significance of the action there. Considerable attention is given to Jesus' words over the bread and wine or even to the bread and wine themselves, but relatively little to the meaning of their distribution and reception. This holds especially for churches with a so-called "low" view of the Lord's Supper: churches that consider it to be primarily a commemoration of Christ's death. Granted, they may also designate it "a means of grace" and may assert that it involves some special "communion" with Christ. But they are hard pressed to be specific, for not much is assumed to be happening other than the worshipers' being inspired by calling to mind the cross. Even the benefits suggested as coming via the Sacrament are only nebulously described as "spiritual" in nature. And at that, the benefits are supposed to be the result of an experience that, basically, is either intellectual or aesthetic or perhaps a mixture of both. So, almost no attention is given to the meaning of the elements' distribution and reception. In fact, for all intents and purposes, worshipers could approach and leave the table without ever partaking of the elements and this "low" view of the Sacrament might still be served. Christ could still be regarded as present for "communion" — is he not always, when two or three assemble in his name? And the congregation, upon hearing the words of institution, would still be reminded of his death.

We have observed, however, that the bread and wine mean what Jesus means in his sacrificial obedience unto death — namely, salvation — and that this significance was attributed to the elements directly in relation to their being offered to the disciples. This, of course, is to say that the Sacrament's meaning must be grasped with respect to the elements' being consumed. These are the eucharistic actions — the blessing and offering of the elements, on the one hand, and the acceptance of them, on the other — without which the Sacrament would be no sacrament. Its vitality includes the words and actions together. And as the bread and wine signify the gift of salvation issuing from Jesus' obedience, *one's faithful consumption of them means one's real reception of that gift and one's equally real involvement in that obedience.* But we have to approach this as Hebrews for it to make any sense.

PROPHETIC SYMBOLISM AND EFFECTIVE REPRESENTATION

Pertinent here are those aspects of ancient practice which Hebraists have called "prophetic symbolism" and "effective representation."

Jesus' words and actions as prophetic symbolism. Israel's prophets often delivered God's word in the way of an enacted parable — a symbolism wherein the dramatization itself was the living, effectual word of the Lord.[1] For example, when Judah misplaced trust in Egypt for deliverance from the Assyrian threat, Isaiah walked barefoot and naked in public, demonstrating the sort of disaster that would befall the Egyptians (Isa. 20:2-6). Jeremiah wore a yoke in the presence of the kings plotting a revolt and told them to submit to the yoke of Nebuchadnezzar; he thus declared that their servitude to Babylon was God's judgment upon them, which they would profit to acknowledge as such (Jer. 27:2-15; cf. ch. 28:10-16).

[1] See H. Wheeler Robinson, "Prophetic Symbolism," *Old Testament Essays* (London: Charles Griffin & Co., Ltd., 1927), pp. 1-17.

Likewise, he broke a jar in the sight of the people and foretold a coming destruction which, since the Lord had spoken,
was as certain as the broken jar (ch. 19:1-11). And Ezekiel
portrayed the "son of man" constructing a miniature of
Jerusalem with siegeworks against it (Ezek. 4:1-3) — an announcement of the city's dread fate.[2]

Jesus' eucharistic words and actions comprised such a symbolism. On numerous occasions he employed the prophetic
method of dramatizing God's word.[3] And he used it at the Last
Supper in a lively, saving proclamation. Referring the broken
bread and outpoured wine to himself, he not only foretold that
his death was imminent and that salvation would issue therefrom but he made that salvation effectual for the disciples,
then and there, by offering it to them. The bread and wine,
signifying him in his obedience unto death, were *given* to the
disciples. That is to say, the significance of his obedience was
itself given to them, actually given to them. The prophets'
symbolism, rooted in their awareness of peculiar relationship
to God, was believed to set in motion the thing it expressed.
Similarly, the intent of Jesus' symbolism was to make salvation
a present reality for the disciples. What he offered them was
not simply knowledge but saving participation; not mere in-
formation about, but involvement in, his sacrificial obedience.
Much more must be said of that.

But at this point a question arises. If the eucharistic words
bespeak a completed sacrifice, an obedience finally sealed in
death, how could Jesus offer the salvation from it as a present
reality *before* his sacrifice was completed? He could only offer
the *meaning* of that sacrifice, the gift of what it would mean

[2] For other instances of prophetic symbolism in Israel, cf. I Kings
11:29-31; 22:11; Isa. 7:3, 14; 8:1-4; Jer. 32:6-15; Ezek. 12:3-16, 17-20;
37:15-28; Hos., chs. 1 to 3.
[3] As in eating with the ungodly (*infra*, pp. 40, 90); riding into Jerusalem and identifying himself with the Temple (*supra*, p. 15); cleansing
the Temple (Matt. 21:12-13; Mark 11:15-18; Luke 19:45-46; John
2:14-16); cursing the fig tree (Matt. 21:18-22; Mark 11:12-14, 20-26);
washing the disciples' feet (John 13:3-11); and the seven " signs " in the
Fourth Gospel (chs. 2:1-11; 4:46-54; 5; 6:1-14, 16-21; 9:1-7; 11:1-44).

once it *was* completed. So in his prophetic symbolism (his eucharistic words and actions together), he said in effect: " This broken bread and outpoured wine mean me as broken to the extent of spilled blood. They mean what my obedience unto death means. They signify salvation, and that is what I now hand to you. Here, receive the gift for what it will mean."

This is to say that the gift was really offered to the disciples. It is a mistake to read *estin* in the eucharistic words as merely " stands for" or "represents." Such an interpretation, in addition to the difficulties noted above,[4] lessens the force of Jesus' offer. It detracts from the effectiveness of his dramatic, prophetic act. Besides, salvation is not what Jesus stands for or represents. It is what he is, what he means, and what he really gives to men.

The effective representation of the gift. Admittedly, the potent sacramentalism implied in this import of Jesus' action is alien to modern thought. Perhaps it is so alien, or so potent, as to appear incredible. But we can at least view it more sympathetically within the framework of " effective representation." That the saving gift of Jesus' obedience might be actually offered through the bread and wine and might be actually appropriated by one's taking the elements — this required for the disciples no new metaphysic. It corresponds, as Rudolf Otto has said,

to an ancient view which was found in many places, and still exists to-day. Never strictly defined, but for that reason only the more vivid, the view is that one can transfer or appropriate the essence, the power, the effect, the peculiar nature, the curse, or the blessing which belongs to a thing or process X by the use of a representative of X. Such a representation becomes effective through the will of him who has control over X.[5]

The idea of effective representation, especially as it bears on the Sacrament, entails the Hebraic concept of the vitality

[4] *Supra,* pp. 26–27.
[5] Rudolf Otto, *The Kingdom of God and the Son of Man,* rev. ed. tr. by Floyd V. Filson and Bertram Lee-Woolf (London: Lutterworth Press, 1943), p. 302.

of the individual.[6] It was conceived as possible for the individual to exude a power beyond himself, affecting the condition of other persons and things. This influence might be extended through one's name,[7] his actions for good or evil,[8] even his property.[9] Exceptionally noteworthy is the fact that the spoken word, when expressive of one's whole being, could be such an extension of the individual's power; particularly, in pronouncing blessings.[10] And when the individual spoke under divine inspiration, his word was believed to be all the more powerful. So Jesus' blessing the elements and relating them to his sacrificial obedience could be thought to make them effective carriers of the saving gift proceeding from that obedience.

Reversing the direction, the individual was also believed to be keenly sensitive to forces outside himself. This assumption lay at the base of Israel's sacrificial system. Because the individual is a psychophysical being, and since no basic dualism separated the material and spiritual in human life, the whole person could be affected by something "purely physical," as we say. Hence, if a man touched a ceremonially unclean person or thing, he was rendered unclean himself. Purification was then required, which usually involved contact with material agents. To such outside influences the individual was constantly accessible. Once again we therefore see how the bread

[6] See two studies by Aubrey R. Johnson: *The One and the Many in the Israelite Conception of God* (Cardiff: University of Wales Press, 1942), pp. 5 ff.; and *The Vitality of the Individual in the Thought of Ancient Israel* (Cardiff: University of Wales Press, 1949).
[7] Enabling him in a sense to live after death; this occasioned the levirate marriage law, designed to keep a man's name from being wiped out (Deut. 25:5-10). Also, the name, besides denoting character, was believed to be charged with a power that speaking it might release (e.g., Amos 6:10); thus do Christians pray in (the power of) Jesus' name.
[8] E.g., Noah's righteousness is seen as operative for his entire household (Gen. 7:1); likewise, Achan's sin is said to have brought death to all in his tent (Josh. 7:22-26).
[9] E.g., the destruction of Achan's possessions, lest his sinful influence continue even after his own removal (Josh. 7:22-26).
[10] E.g., Isaac's blessing of Jacob, which he could not retract even though he had been duped into giving it (Gen. 27:30-38).

and wine could be deemed genuinely effective carriers of the gift issuing from Jesus' obedience.

Let us make quick notice, however, that in no way could they be regarded as effective *in themselves*. The efficacy of Jesus' prophetic symbolism at the Supper depended upon his own willful declaration and action. In his peculiar relation to God, *he* charged the elements with their new significance; and in distributing them, *he* freely offered the gift. Moreover, in order to receive the gift, the disciples had to act in faith.

EATING AND DRINKING AS AN ACTION OF FAITH

The redemptive meaning of Jesus' obedience unto death was sacramentally received by the disciples through their faithful eating and drinking. Here too we encounter something that cannot be appreciated without reference to Hebraic thought and practice. We must take into account the Hebrew significance of eating and drinking, and apply it to the situation at hand.

The Hebrew significance. That significance may be summarized under three main considerations. First, a particular fellowship could be established through eating and drinking, especially when it was done "before Yahweh" or as a religious act. To dine with another was to be brought into intimate relationship with him. It established a common bond, a covenantal fellowship of mutual obligations. For instance, Israel is reported to have effected an alliance with the Gibeonites in partaking of their victuals (Josh. 9:3-15). Though God had not sanctioned it and though the people of Gibeon had covenanted under false pretenses, Israel could not rescind the alliance, but was bound to come to their aid (chs. 9:16 ff.; 10:1 ff.).

The notion is again dramatized in the Judean messenger sent to Jeroboam with a word of judgment. After delivering it, he refused the king's shrewd invitation to dine, saying:

If you give me half your house, I will not go in with you. And I will not eat bread or drink water in this place; for so was it commanded me by the word of the LORD, saying, "You shall neither eat bread, nor drink water, nor return by the way that you came." (I Kings 13:8-9.)

In other words, Judah, whom the messenger represents, will have nothing to do with the Northern Kingdom. Likewise, the prophets of Baal and Asherah against whom Elijah strove were said to be those " who eat at Jezebel's table " (I Kings 18:19) — the author's emphatic way of asserting the queen's oneness with them. So too the psalmist's complaint: " Even my bosom friend in whom I trusted, who ate of my bread, has lifted his heel against me " (Ps. 41:9). It was the last act of treachery, to break the bonds of a table fellowship. Small wonder Jesus repeated the word concerning Judas (John 13:18).

This effecting of intimacy between men through eating and drinking was understood to include their fellowship with God. It could hardly be otherwise in Israelite theology, since the covenant terms stipulated that one's relationship with the Lord is inseparable from one's human relationships. And ancients in general believed that dining with men of another cult established bonds with their god.[11] This underlay the boast attributed to Esther, that she had not eaten at Haman's table but had remained loyal to Yahweh (Additions to Esth. 14:17). It is explicit in the acceptance of Jethro into Israel's cult. Upon hearing of the exodus, he offered sacrifices to God and then, with Aaron and the elders, ate bread before him (Ex. 18:12).

Hence, to eat or drink what was blessed in God's name or first offered to him meant to be united in his fellowship. The outstanding Old Testament example is the covenanting at Sinai, where the arrangements were formally concluded with Israel's leaders going up into the mountain: " They beheld God, and ate and drank " (ch. 24:11). In other words, Israel

---

[11] Cf. Paul's warning (I Cor. 10:14-22) against eating food offered to idols: idols are not real, but demons are; and to join in pagan worship, wherein demons operate, is to be united with them.

is the people that have dined in God's presence: their relationship with him in the covenant is uniquely intimate!

Second, the Hebrew believed that divine gifts might be imparted through eating and drinking. Fellowship with God is of course the greatest of these. But what is in mind here is the reception of more specific blessings.

The basis of this was the conviction that God, as Giver and Sustainer of life, provides all that is necessary for life. To have an abundant or even barely adequate supply of food and drink was therefore taken as a sign of his favor.[12] Hosea thus complained of Israel's sometime stupidity in supposing that other gods were furnishing bread and water (Hos. 2:5, 8). Conversely, to be without sustenance was a sign of God's displeasure. Amos, for one, was astounded when the people, plagued with cleanness of teeth in all their cities, failed to heed the sign and repent (Amos 4:6-9). At times, to be sure, the idea was taken too far. The Deuteronomic teaching — that all sin results in suffering — was occasionally reversed to say all suffering is the result of sin; then *all* want of food was to be proof of judgment.[13] But at other times, in sight of wholesale disobedience, famine could be a legitimate figure of God's wrath. For he is the One who controls what is needed for life to continue.

The specific blessings seen as coming often through eating and drinking were what we would call redemptive and sometimes charismatic: forgiveness, cleansing, knowledge of God's will, and the like. For example, the Aaronic priests were to be ordained and consecrated in eating the sacrifices with which atonement was made (Ex. 29:33). The food here sanctifies by being consumed. Priestly consumption of sin offerings was to have a similar effect in behalf of the people. Hence, it is said, Moses was outraged when Aaron's sons failed to eat their portion of an offering, and berated them:

---

[12] Cf. Joel 2:18 ff.; Deut. 32:13-14; Neh. 9:20; Ps. 78:24-29; 107:9; 111:5.

[13] An error the Bible seeks to correct; e.g., Job 15:23, putting it on the lips of Eliphaz.

Why have you not eaten the sin offering in the place of the sanctuary, since it is a thing most holy and has been given to you that you may bear the iniquity of the congregation, to make atonement for them before the LORD? (Lev. 10:17.)

Since atoning forgiveness might be so imparted, it was second nature for the psalmist to confess, "The LORD is my chosen portion and my cup" (Ps. 16:5); and again, "I will lift up the cup of salvation" (Ps. 116:13). Even God's word could come to one through eating, as when Ezekiel envisioned the "son of man" being commanded to eat the scroll (Ezek. 3:1-3).

Now, of course, some of the Old Testament's references along this line are figurative, as is Ezek. 3:1-3. But all of them are not, and this explains whatever figurative references one finds: the Hebrew really believed that particular blessings *could be* and often *were* imparted through eating and drinking. And that is just the point.

But many are ready to object that all this seems to be little more than "mechanical sacramentalism" — a paganlike magic assumed to function *ex opere operato,* a business in which the god is manipulated for favors. This leads to the third consideration, namely, such eating and drinking as were supposed to be media of establishing communion with God and means of obtaining gifts from him had to be done within the context of obedient faith. Keeping with Israelite theology, Hebrew sacramentalism allowed no proper room for anything mechanical. It was believed ordained by God, was carried out in answer to his command, and was to be accompanied by repentance. Its effectiveness basically depended upon him who was Israel's Redeemer, the Creator-Lord who cannot be controlled by the doings of any creature. Manipulating him was out of the question.

To engage in a sacramental rite was rather to acknowledge the fundamental terms of the covenant, grace and response to grace: God acts in grace to bless his people, they respond in obedience to receive the blessing. Those who ate the sacrifices were those whom he had saved in the exodus and whom he was graciously maintaining as his chosen ones. Their act itself was in response to his initiating mercy. Even the Passover meal in Egypt, which was antecedent to the actual deliverance, was the product of his initiative. It was his idea to begin with, and not something that otherwise persuaded him to move in the Hebrews' behalf. Participation in Passover observance, at first and ever after, was thus considered to be a faithful following of God's directive.

The requirement that sacramental eating and drinking be done in faith, in obedient response to God's redemptive lordship, accounts for the harsh judgments against violations of it. On the one hand, again citing the Passover, the man who refused to eat it was to be cut off from the nation (Num. 9:13). Such defiance regarding appointed feasts would be a flat denial of what all Israelites are — God's own people (therefore, eating before him) living in fellowship with him. On the other hand, he who kept the feasts, but apart from righteous conduct in daily affairs, did what is an abomination to the Lord (Isa. 1:12-14). Such a man lies, acting as though he is faithful when in truth he is not. In the sanctuary he pretends to say yes to God's word, whereas out in the street he says no to it. Paul thus accused the Corinthians, who were acting *as if* they were eating the Lord's Supper, of *not* eating it (I Cor. 11:20). Not that the ritual was confused, but their careless attitude had rendered it worthless (v. 21). In fact, one who so desecrates the Sacrament eats and drinks judgment upon himself — heavy judgment, the kind that may even result in sickness and death (vs. 27-30)!

Now this sacramentalism is not the pagan, mechanical type. It finds its effectiveness primarily in nothing that man himself does, yet it necessarily requires his obedience. Its main concern is not how people are made to feel by the liturgy or lighting or background music, but what is done by the Lord to redeem them. And this is precisely the type of sacramentalism blessed to a people who are forever and in all things dependent on God.

The significance in Jesus' day. That the Hebrew significance of eating and drinking carried into the Christian era is witnessed in the intertestamental and New Testament literature. Counsel is given in Ecclus. 9:16 to eat with only the upright, and in Manual of Discipline 5:16-17 to eat or drink nothing belonging to an impure man. According to the latter document, participation in the communal meal, which might be withheld two years for disciplinary reasons, signified full membership in the Qumran community (ch. 7:19). Covenantal fellowship was effected and maintained thus, at table.

Moving into the Gospels, we come upon the frequently recorded complaint that Jesus ate with publicans and sinners.[14] The Pharisees recognized that he was thereby intimately identifying with these folk and was according them a place in God's purpose. His answer to the objection was that the sick, not the healthy, need a doctor and that he had come not to call the righteous but sinners. Jesus' action in taking the ungodly as table companions was calculated. It was a dramatic self-announcement that here was the Servant of the Lord who would be "numbered with the transgressors" (Isa. 53:12). He *dined* with them! Not because he found their company attractive; not because he wanted them to suppose they were less despicable than public opinion had it; not because he merely felt sorry for them and wanted to boost their morale. He dined with them: (1) because in their overt depravity they especially represented — as a law-abiding Jew could not — everyone who was sinful before God; and (2) because he was that Servant in redemption who was to be identified with all such men. That is why *he* dined with *them*.

This Hebrew belief about eating and drinking also explains why the Judaizing party took Peter to task for his visit in the home of Cornelius. The problem was not that he had preached to Gentiles, which may have been suspect, but that he had eaten with them, which was unthinkable (Acts 11:2-3). Peter had allowed himself, a Jew, to be brought into binding relationship with uncircumcised men!

[14] Matt. 9:11; 11:19; Mark 2:16; Luke 5:30; 7:34; 15:2; 19:7.

Further, we recall the apostle's exhortation to the Corinthians (I Cor. 10:14-22) to shun the worship of idols, lest by partaking of the table of demons they be made partners with demons.[15] Moreover, it was assumed that when believers ate of the one sacramental loaf, they were united together in Christ, just as those who ate Israel's sacrifices were made partners in God (vs. 17-18).

So there is no question that the Hebrew significance of eating and drinking prevailed in the thinking of Jesus and his church. We profit to remember, however, that such eating and drinking, whereby communion with God was established and divine gifts were received, had to be done in obedient faith. To do otherwise was to live a lie, profaning Christ's body and blood, and thus to incur judgment (ch. 11:27-30).

The meaning at the Last Supper. It remains now to translate the above meaning of eating and drinking into the terms of Jesus' eucharistic behavior and the disciples' response. This must be done with a view to the historical situation and the necessity of a corporate atonement.

The significance of Jesus' obedience unto death, denoted in the broken bread and outpoured wine, was effectively represented as a gift in his distributing the elements for the disciples to consume. That, we have seen, meant the gift of Jesus himself in his completed sacrifice: in other words, God's great gift of salvation. This was offered, and this was received. The gift, with its numerous implications, was appropriated through faithful eating and drinking. This is really all that was done in the sacramental action at the Supper. Nothing more could have possibly been done.

At the same time, this import of the action at the Last Supper was qualified by the occasion. The cross, though central in Jesus' mind, was still a future event, at least some hours away. The finished sacrifice of his obedience, prefigured in the condition of the bread and wine, was yet unfinished. Consequently, the overall significance of the proffered gift could

[15] Cf. note 11 above.

not at the moment be realized in full. To be sure, the gift of
salvation was received in the disciples' consumption of the
elements. Its effects, however, could be only partially realized.
Expiation of sin and once-for-all forgiveness, the final end
of atoning sacrifice in the fulfillment of sacrifice, the establishment of the new age and God's righteous rule in conquer-
ing sin and death — these things depended (1) on the Servant's being poured out, which by Jesus' own definition meant
his being emptied in death; (2) on God's raising him to new
life; and (3) on God's endowing the church with the Holy
Spirit. These things were still to come. But the effect of God's
gift in Christ that *was* presently realized by the disciples made
the remaining effects a certainty for them.

On this point we must speak of the disciples' common fellowship in Jesus himself, their "communion" with him.
Through eating and drinking the elements, they were united
in him and with him. For, in the Hebrew view, those who eat
bread together are commonly joined to the one who presents
it. In other words, the disciples were given a participation in
Jesus' sacrifice. Being united with him, they would take part in
it themselves. They would share in that obedience unto death
which the bread and wine signified and which was on the
verge of being completed — would really share in it!

That the disciples might do so, that it could be deemed even
possible, involves a phase of Hebrew psychology known as
corporate personality.[16] It will do for us to look at the concept
in some detail, taking concrete examples from both Old and
New Testaments, since it is strange to modern ears and since
the atonement itself is at stake here. Moreover, we ought to in-
struct our people in the concept, not only to prepare them for
Communion but also let them know the deeper meaning in
their being called "communicants."

---

[16] Classically treated by H. Wheeler Robinson, "The Hebrew Conception of Corporate Personality," *Werden und Wesen des Alten Testaments*, ed. by Paul Volz, Friedrich Stummer, and Johannes Hempel
(Berlin: Alfred Töpplemann, 1936), pp. 49–62.

In Semitic thought generally, and Hebraic thought particularly, the group rather than the individual constituted the basic unit of personality. The individual, for all his vitality, was considered to be essentially a corporate being, a person whose existence and very life were engulfed in that of the group. This of course did not preclude a genuine importance being accorded him in Old Testament religion. The patriarchs were esteemed great men one by one. Moses' name was that of a hero, as were those of certain judges and kings, each of whom played his distinctive role in Israel's history and faith. The psalmists and prophets are other eminent examples of individual communion with God. And the law, keeping with the later prophetic reemphasis on each man's responsibility before God, gave increased attention to individual guilt and need. Even so, the individual was not held apart as an entity in himself. Rather, he was believed to be so integrally related to the group that what any of its members did directly implicated him.

For instance, the story of Achan's disobedience. When he snatched a bit of the Jericho spoil for his own, after it had been declared taboo, his guilt extended to the entire people, bringing national disaster and provoking the judgment,

> *Israel* has sinned; *they* have transgressed my covenant which I commanded them; *they* have taken some of the devoted things; *they* have stolen, and lied, and put them among *their* own stuff. (Josh. 7:11.)

Here again is a vast difference between Hebrew and Greek. In Greek thought a man's body (*sōma*) sets him off from others, allowing him the possibility of a hermit. But Hebrew does not even have a word corresponding to *sōma* in this sense. Instead, all mankind is *bâsar* (flesh); hence,

> The flesh-body was not what partitioned a man off from his neighbour; it was rather what bound him in the bundle of life with all men and nature, so that he could never make his unique answer to

God as an isolated individual, apart from his relation to his neighbour.[17]

This corporate solidarity of mankind gets notable expression in the first creation narrative, where it is said that God created not *a* man but *'ādām* — i.e., " man." And notice the parallelism: " In the image of God he created *him;* male and female he created *them* " (Gen. 1:27) — "them" equals "him"! The many are thus one mankind. The idea is found also in the J narrative, where *ha-'ādām*, " the man," is represented by an individual; but, significantly, a corporate individual. He is the stuff out of which the woman is made (ch. 2:21-24); hence a one-flesh humanity. And it is this one-flesh, corporate humanity which is to be seen in Gen., ch. 3, as involved in the Fall.

Mankind's real corporateness is the only adequate base for proceeding to the Scriptural teaching of that otherwise theological bugaboo, " original " sin. Since Israelite faith in Yahweh as creator would not permit belief in an originally bad creation, there had to be some explanation for the sorry condition of Israel and the world. What could it be? Simply this: *ha-'ādām* had sinned and, in so doing, had involved everyone thereafter in the deed. Despair and death would ensue for all — because mankind is a corporate body, one *bâsar*, a psychophysical unity. This is to say, when " Adam " sinned, we were there! That the Hebrews retained this view of a corporately corrupt humanity is certain from Paul's matter-of-fact reference to it: he takes for granted the universal effect of one man's sin and argues therefrom the universal effect of another Man's righteousness (Rom. 5:12-21).

In its concern with salvation, however, the Bible speaks not only of a corporate race but also of another group: the people of God, set apart from the world. This latter, elect group is also corporate in nature, its members being joined in what I should

---

[17] John A. T. Robinson, *The Body: A Study in Pauline Theology* (London: SCM Press, Ltd., 1952), p. 15.

have to call a real, organic unity.[18] If the nation Israel is real
and if Israelites are really members of it, then their union must
be organic; for, as we have noted, Hebrew thought made no
fundamental distinction between the physical and spiritual in
human life. Israel is a body, not an idea.

A particularly instructive case to point up Israel's oneness
is the numbering of those who are said to have come out of
Egypt: around six hundred thousand able-bodied men (Ex.
12:37; Num. 1:17-46; 26:1-56). To this figure must be added
the old men, women, and children — all of which would total
over two million people, plus their cattle! That this is clean
beyond reason is demonstrated in the calculations of an ex-
staff officer who, from his professional knowledge, indicates
that

such a multitude, walking five abreast, with their cattle, would be
likely to make an average speed of a mile an hour, and would take
230 hours to pass a given point; would need, on rations sufficient
for bare subsistence, 900 tons of food (two train loads) per day,
2,400 tons of firewood daily for cooking, and so on.[19]

Whereas it is generally believed that between two and six
thousand made the actual journey, the figure of six hundred
thousand fighting men may represent a later census, perhaps
one taken in David's reign (II Sam. 24:1 ff.). In any event, as
Gabriel Hebert observes,[20] it stands for the whole nation and
is meant to say that all Israelites, being a corporate body, participated in the deliverance themselves. When God redeemed
his people long ago, the later generations were there.[21] Israel
is basically one.

[18] Being a modern Western man, I am at a loss to explain the reality
of this in any way so as to comprehend it; but if I were an ancient Hebrew man, who was not given to systematic formulations, I would
neither need nor try to explain it.
[19] Reported by Gabriel Hebert, *When Israel Came Out of Egypt* (John
Knox Press, 1961), pp. 82–83.
[20] *Ibid.*, pp. 83–85.
[21] So the words attributed to Moses, speaking at the end of the wilderness period to all those about to enter Canaan, although *only two* of
them are said to have been among the original generation of Israel: " But

The New Testament teaching about the nature of God's people is no different, except for their being a " new " Israel, founded in a new deliverance. The church is the body of Christ, whose members are as inseparably related to one another as are the members of a human body (I Cor. 12:12-26). Just as redemption in the Old Testament is corporate, meaning membership in the nation Israel, salvation according to the New is only within the body of Christ. Not because God is fussy about one's " joining " the church. It is simply the fact of the matter: the redeemed man is *in* Christ with all the rest of the redeemed, they *are* members of one body. At the profoundest level of our being, we are communicants with Christ and thus with one another. Hence, " If one member suffers, all suffer together; if one member is honored, all rejoice together " (ch. 12:26). Israel is still basically one.

Therefore, following this concept of corporate personality, it was quite possible for the disciples actually to participate in Jesus' obedience. The many could be regarded as really involved in the act of the one (cf. Rom. 6:1-11).

The primary effect, then, of the disciples' reception of the gift of salvation at the Supper was a share in Jesus' sacrifice. Eating and drinking what he offered them, they were united with him, were given a share in his obedience unto death. And being really united with him, they were certain to receive the full effects of the gift, once that obedience unto death was finished and God established the new age in power.

NECESSARY INVOLVEMENT IN JESUS' OBEDIENCE

Not only *did* the disciples receive a share in Jesus' obedience unto death but it was necessary that they should. The

---

the LORD has taken you, and brought you forth out of the iron furnace, out of Egypt, to be a people of his own possession, as at this day " (Deut. 4:20). So also was the Passover service to be explained each year: " And you shall tell your son on that day, ' It is because of what the LORD did for me when I came out of Egypt ' " (Ex. 13:8).

fact will reappear in our next chapter, yet it warrants particular notice here in relation to this effect at the Supper.

For Jesus' sacrificial life and death to be a true fulfillment of God's covenanting with Israel and giving sacrifice for atonement, the people Jesus would redeem would have to be personally involved with him. On the one hand, those for whom a sacrifice was made were regarded as necessarily associated somehow with the sacrificial victim. The worshiper might be directed, for example, to touch the victim. When it was then slain or driven from the camp, he was identified with it in what its death or departure represented for atonement (cf. Lev. 1:4; 3:2, 8, 13; 16:21).

When a covenant was ratified, identification with the victim seems to have been especially necessary. As the author of Hebrews put it, " Where a covenant [22] is involved, the death of the one who made it must be established " (Heb. 9:16). This is to say that we must share Christ's sacrificial death if we are to be partners in his new covenant. This probably reflects the ancient idea that, since only a dead man can be utterly trusted never to renege his word, both parties to a contract or covenant had to be represented as dying. Therefore,

the New Covenant carries with it the assurance of its own permanent validity, for it was consecrated by the death of One who represented both contracting parties, One who bears the double title and the double nature, of Son of God and Son of Man, the man, Christ Jesus.[23]

To paraphrase the Negro spiritual, " We were there when they crucified our Lord." We had to be!

On the other hand, involvement in Jesus' obedience was necessitated by God's demand that his people be fully righteous. Redemptive obedience, like that of the Servant Christ, lay at the heart of the covenant theology: Abraham would

---

[22] *Diathēkē,* often translated " will " in this text; but in addition to the commentaries, see Douglas McLaren, " The Feast of the New Covenant," *Church Quarterly Review,* 115:1-9 (Oct., 1932).
[23] *Ibid.,* p. 9.

be a blessing to the nations in being the father of a faithful people (Gen. 12:1-3). God's demand always was that Israel be obedient — and Jesus did not come down the road to alleviate that with news of a lesser righteousness. He rather voiced the demand in more stringent terms than ever, telling his disciples they must be perfect (*teleios*, i.e., full, accomplished) even as God is perfect! In other words, as the context of Matt. 5:48 makes clear, Israel must be complete, must realize her destined personality in self-sacrificial love, and thereby serve as the image of God. But how in the world could this demand ever be met? Only in Jesus, as he promised it would be: he came, he said, not to destroy the Law and the Prophets but to fulfill them to the last jot and tittle (Matt. 5:17-18; cf. Luke 16:17). And so they *are* fulfilled. Being in him, having participated in his utterly self-sacrificial obedience, we really *are* righteous and loving. God can count us so in Christ, without having to close his eyes to our otherwise rebellious nature and behavior.

There is a certain vulgarity in our preaching and teaching about the atonement when this fact is overlooked. Much is said about penal substitution (as it should be!), and we are grateful beyond words that Jesus shouldered the burden of our sin. But when Paul is heard to say that we are justified by faith and reckoned as righteous, the usual explanation given is that God simply acts *as if* we were righteous, though of course we are not. But pretending is pretending, merely make-believe even when spoken of God. We need not speak of him that way — we must not speak that way. Just as Paul's theology of the atonement entails our real union with Christ, and just as faith is a personal relationship with Christ, so are we to believe that Jesus' satisfaction of God's demand for righteousness is ours as well. His act, in view of the meaning he gave it at the Last Supper and elsewhere, was necessarily a corporate act — an act in which his people acted in him and with him. Otherwise, had his obedience not really involved us, justification would be injustice, with God's Torah still unfulfilled, and the atonement would be immoral, in its being simply the punishment of the Just for the unjust.

So what was done in terms of the disciples' sacramental eating and drinking *had* to be done. They were offered and they received in faith the covenant gift of salvation in union with Christ, a share in his obedience unto death. That is what they needed — real, redemptive involvement with him — not just an injection of spiritual strength to help them through a crisis.

III JESUS' FULFILLMENT OF OLD TESTAMENT SACRIFICE

Before considering how the meaning of the Last Supper carried into the early church's practice, we should note what the accounts of the Supper indicate about Jesus' fulfillment of Old Testament sacrifice.

Fulfillment is the key word to describe the New Testament's relation to the Old. Nowhere is this more apparent than in what the upper room reveals about the fullness of Jesus' sacrificial work. The Passover, Israel's system of sacrifices, Second Isaiah's hope for a Suffering Servant, the covenant-making at Sinai, and Jeremiah's promise of a new covenant — all this is declared at the Last Supper to be fulfilled in Jesus' sacrifice and our corporate involvement with him. There is a richness here that we would do well to draw upon when inviting men to the Lord's Table. Further, to study this theme of fulfillment, distinctly as it relates to Jesus' eucharistic words and actions, is to gain a keener appreciation of the historical significance of the upper room event for the church — i.e., not merely the institution of a Christian sacrament but the inauguration of a new Israel.

In Terms of the Passover

Fulfillment of Old Testament sacrifice is seen, first of all, in terms of the Passover. There is reason to believe that Jesus compared himself to the Passover lamb. The so-called "Pauline" *Passa-Haggadha,* or explanation of Passover ritual (I Cor. 5:7-8), which speaks of "Christ, our paschal lamb," was evidently not a new idea with Paul. Mentioning it but incidentally, he assumed that the Corinthians were familiar with the comparison. What are probably abbreviated references to a Christian *Passa-Haggadha* are found in I Peter 1:19 and Rev. 5:6, 9, 12; 12:11. Moreover, the comparison is unmistakable in the Fourth Gospel's dating of the crucifixion on Nisan 14, making Jesus' death coincide with that of the Passover lambs being slain in the Temple. Hence the Johannine announcement of Jesus as the Lamb of God (John 1:29, 36), and the observation that none of his bones was broken (ch. 19:36), which is in signal accord with regulations for treatment of the paschal victim (Ex. 12:46; Num. 9:12).

This comparison most likely originated at the Last Supper itself. The fact that Jesus related the unleavened bread and third Passover cup to himself suggests that he must have spoken also of the paschal victim with reference to himself. The Synoptic tradition of the Supper implies such a comparison. It identifies the meal as a Passover and, at the same time, centers attention on the cross. This is to say in effect that *Jesus'* sacrifice is the correct focus for paschal observance. The Johannine dating of the crucifixion, which seems to follow the official calendar,[1] may have been an effort to make explicit this comparison already implied in the Synoptic tradition. It is, of course, true that the annual paschal sacrifice in Jesus' day was not considered an atonement for sin. But he, of all men, would have felt least restricted by that. An early comparison between him and the Passover lamb *was* made, and we know he viewed his death, at the Last Supper particularly, as efficacious for sin.

In any event, new meaning was given to the Passover, notably *in the way opened up by the Passover's own nature.* It

---

[1] In regard to the paschal character of the Last Supper and the conflicting Synoptic and Johannine chronologies, see Appendix D.

was the most basic sacrifice of Israel's cultus. Granted, it had primitive origins in earlier Semitic religion, as did the whole sacrificial system. But in the Passover's meaning for Israel, as a nation, Semitic antecedents take a second seat. Not because antecedents are unimportant, but because the Passover was inseparably tied to the fundamental event in the nation's life — the exodus. Instituted on the eve of Israel's redemption, it became the standing commemoration of her deliverance and creation as God's people.[2] The slaying of the victim, the meal following, and the explanation of the proceedings composed a powerful remembering. Eating as ones ready for a journey — standing [3] with staff in hand, feet shod, loins girded — the celebrants were reminded that they themselves had been liberated along with their fathers of old and established as God's elect: "And you shall tell your son on that day, 'It is because of what the LORD did for me when I came out of Egypt'" (Ex. 13:8). Historically and theologically, therefore, the Passover was the sacrifice of first importance.

This uniqueness of the Passover was maintained in the development of the sacrificial system. There were three main classes of animal sacrifice: sin and guilt offerings, burnt offerings, peace offerings.[4] With each of these the Passover had marked similarities, but was never exclusively identified with any one of them. Although its special resemblance to the peace offerings may have caused it to be associated with them, at certain points the Passover came to resemble the entire Jewish sacrificial ritual, yet properly remained distinct.

The upshot of all this is that the Old Testament sacrificial ritual points to its own completion in the Passover *particularly*.

[2] Passover enactments are found in Ex. 12:1-27, 43-49; 13:3-16; 23:15; 34:18, 25; Lev. 23:5-8; Num. 28:16-25; Deut. 16:1-18; Ezek. 45:21-24.
[3] But by Jesus' day the custom was to recline, symbolizing the Jews' freedom under God.
[4] The sin offerings (Lev. 4:1 to 5:13) and guilt offerings (chs. 5:14 to 6:7; 7:1-7; Num. 5:5-8) were much alike, and in Lev. 5:6 seem identical. In regard to burnt offerings, see Lev., chs. 1; 6:9-13; for peace offerings, chs. 3; 7:11-18.

Attributing historical and theological priority to the Passover, Israel's cultus opens the door for the New Testament expression of Christ our paschal Lamb. By its unique position in Israelite worship, the Passover declares that what is needed for sacrifice to be perfected is deliverance. And that is exactly what we meet in the Lamb "who takes away the sin of the world!" (John 1:29.) He liberates his people in a new deliverance — and a mightier enemy than Pharaoh was here! And a mightier deliverance too. The sin of the *world* is removed in *this* Lamb! Israel's sacrificial system is thus brought to its eschatological end.

So the Passover, which was neither sin nor guilt offering, nor burnt offering, nor peace offering, but which bore likenesses to each of them, becomes in Christ their whole fulfillment. In him the ultimate significance of Israel's Passover, her commemoration of the exodus redemption, is unveiled. And this is why the Synoptic accounts of the Supper name the meal a Passover, yet make Jesus' sacrifice the central thing: he does not find his meaning in Israel's Passover; rather, Israel's Passover finds its full meaning in him!

Behold, the Lamb!

IN TERMS OF SECOND ISAIAH'S "SERVANT"

Fulfillment of Old Testament sacrifice is expressed even more emphatically in terms of Second Isaiah's "Servant of the Lord." At the Last Supper, Jesus was fairly absorbed with thoughts of the Servant's mission. The wine saying speaks of his blood as "*poured out* for *many*" (Mark 14:24). And in the so-called Suffering Servant poem we read: "He *poured out* himself [his *nephesh*] [5] to death, and was numbered with the transgressors; yet he bore the sin of *many*" (Isa. 53:12). The note of forgiveness implied here was made explicit in the Matthean expansion, "Unto forgiveness of sins" (Matt. 26:28). And according to Luke 22:37, just prior to leaving for the

[5] For this meaning of *nephesh*, often translated "soul," see *supra*, p. 18.

Mount of Olives, Jesus again applied Isa. 53:12 to himself: "For I tell you that this scripture must be fulfilled in me, 'And he was reckoned with transgressors.'"

What is the meaning of Jesus' sacrifice in terms of the Suffering Servant? To put it in a word, as we come upon that meaning at the Last Supper: the mission of the "many," if but a remnant, is fulfilled in the mission of the "One" on behalf of the "many."

Now let us dig into this meaning, first by entertaining briefly a critical question: that of the Servant's identity. The Servant in Second Isaiah seems primarily to be a corporate figure, meaning Israel. It is, of course, clear that the identity shifts back and forth between the nation as a whole and the nation as a remnant. Exegetical grounds are wanting, however, for a necessarily "individualist" interpretation of the Servant poems themselves (Isa. 42:1-4; 49:1-6; 50:4-9; 52:13 to 53:12). The so-called fluid concept of the Servant's identity, classically defined by C. R. North and held by countless others,[6] should therefore be viewed with caution when it comes to an individual being in the prophet's mind. The fact — and this is recognized by all, regardless of their final positions — is that the Servant is referred to in standard corporate terms.[7] They are under the figure of an individual, to be sure, but they are nevertheless regularly accepted corporate terms.

The common objection to simply a corporate identity, especially in the Suffering Servant poem (chs. 52:13 to 53:12), is that it would have been an unrealistic expectation for even a holy remnant nation. But this objection really defeats itself. Granted, the figure in chs. 52:13 to 53:12 completely outstrips everything Israel had been in her purest past and everything she could reasonably hope to be in the future. But, the figure was quite beyond anything that could be expected of an in-

[6] Christopher R. North, *The Suffering Servant in Deutero-Isaiah* (London: Oxford University Press, 1948), pp. 193–219.
[7] But in Isa., chs. 49:1-6 and 50:4-9, the Servant speaks in the first person, leading some to conclude that Second Isaiah had himself in mind.

dividual either! In this sense, the hope was unrealistic on both counts.

Yet, it was not. And herein is why we have engaged the moot question of the Servant's identity. Like the future hope of all the prophets, Second Isaiah's was founded in, and was the active word of, the Lord. An eschatological hope, it presumed a new creation, a day when Israel would be God's people in fact (chs. 51:16; 65:17-19). The time itself cried out for redemption if the divine purpose was to meet with success. Jerusalem was lying in ruins, Jacob drenched in disgrace. The Babylonians had invaded the land and ruthlessly prevailed, leaving Judah a calamitous contradiction in terms: a fallen and enslaved people of God. But despite the hopelessly demoralizing situation — not at all dissimilar to what had existed under the Pharaoh — another beginning awaited the nation: a " new " exodus, no less! God would again deliver them from bondage, would make a path for them in the sea and wilderness, and feed them along the way (chs. 40:3-5; 41:18-19; 43:16-19; 48:21; 49:10-11). This time, via the Servant, God's righteous rule would extend throughout the earth (ch. 42:2-4)! So the hope for a Suffering Servant, again like all Old Testament hope which was projected into the end-time, constituted a hope for a " new " covenant, a fully new and right relationship between God and his people. That would be *his* doing, same as the announcement itself was his. All of it rested on his initiative and the eternal sureness of his purpose in calling Israel in the first place.

Now when this is remembered, one is certainly free to conclude that chs. 52:13 to 53:12 *could* have been spoken of a holy nation, as of a holy individual. More importantly, it *had* to be spoken of the nation, at least in the sense of including the nation. From the outset, God's covenant demand was that Israel be his servant in redemption, which our Lord himself understood to mean self-sacrifice for Israel.[8] Surely, that demand could not be sidestepped. The Servant's role was

---

[8] See *supra,* pp. 47–48, concerning Gen. 12:1-3 and Matt. 5:48.

nothing other than the nation's calling.

Is it not possible, then, that the individualist interpretation of the Suffering Servant in Second Isaiah is the product largely of a scholarship that has seen the amazing fulfillment in Jesus? Dr. North admits as much for himself when he says, "I find it hard to believe that the Prophet in his moments of deepest insight intended one thing and the Holy Spirit another." [9]

However that may be, it *was* in the "One" that this hope for the "many" was realized. Still — and this is the point to take home — his mission was to be, indeed must be, their mission as well. They themselves had to be involved in it. And so we see Jesus at the Last Supper extending his own Servant identity to include more than just himself. He offers to the disciples, *and corporately through them offers to all God's people,* a share in his own Servant sacrifice. They faithfully eat and drink the elements he presents to signify his obedience unto death, and they are thereby united with him in it. So also are we. Since the church is forever one body, we acted corporately along with the disciples in their acceptance of a share in Jesus' sacrificial obedience. Israel's role as God's Servant is thus fulfilled in the "many" being joined to that One who would complete his redemptive suffering on a cross!

Finally, Jesus' fulfillment of the Servant's mission regards his acting *on behalf of* the "many" — in other words, his acting vicariously.

Second Isaiah's hope, anticipating a kind of once-for-all atonement, presupposed the limitations of Israel's sacrificial system.[10] The system itself witnessed to its own shortcomings. On the one hand, there were sins for which no sacrifice was prescribed. Murder and adultery fell in this class. A man guilty of one or the other might be forgiven, as was David in his affair with Bathsheba and removal of her husband (II

[9] North, *op. cit.,* p. 219.
[10] Cf. H. H. Rowley, "The Meaning of Sacrifice in the Old Testament," *Bulletin of the John Rylands Library,* 33:97-110 (Sept., 1950), substance of which I use freely.

Sam. 12:13). But evidence is lacking that it was thought all such sins would be forgiven, on the spot, even if penitence was made. From the sinner's standpoint, at least, he had no assurance of forgiveness in every such case. Also, when forgiveness came without a sacrifice prescribed, God's willful judgment was not believed to be definitely canceled. Not only natural consequences but even directly imposed hardships might still ensue. Though Nathan told David he would get by with his life, he also delivered grief to the king: " Nevertheless, because by this deed you have utterly scorned the Lord, the child that is born to you shall die " (v. 14). Provisions were wanting for an effective " covering " of these sins. In excluding them from its province, the Old Testament sacrificial system, which viewed the problem of sin most seriously, indeed with horror, acknowledged its own inability to meet the problem fully.

Nor could it meet the problem finally; for, on the other hand, there was continual repetition of sacrifices. The repetition indicated, at one and the same time, the vitality of the cultus and its outstanding weakness. Sacrifices were offered repeatedly simply because they were considered to be charged with power. Yet, the power was insufficient to produce lasting results. Continual sacrificing was therefore necessary; the system contained no final solution to the problem addressed. Whereas we now have a Priest who, having offered his single sacrifice, was able to sit down at God's hand, the priests of old Israel had to stand at their service daily, offering the same sacrifices again and again (Heb. 10:11-12). One can imagine that it was a wearisome, boring business. Its job was never done; in fact, did not even show signs of progress.

Second Isaiah's suffering prophecy takes these limitations of Israel's cultus to heart. The Servant's sacrifice would accomplish what the established sacrifices could not: a forgiveness in the way of being once and for all. In bearing the iniquity of us all (Isa. 53:6) and pouring out himself to death (v. 12), the Servant would make a vicarious sacrifice of universal significance — a sacrifice issuing in salvation for Israel and the nations (ch. 49:6), a sacrifice with meaning for all.

It cannot, of course, be said that the prophet envisioned a once-for-all sacrifice precisely as it was worked out in Christ. This would be all the more true if he was thinking of its accomplishment primarily through a segment of the nation and not an individual. Nonetheless, he did envision its being operative for all the sins and sinfulness of everyone to be redeemed. And especially with regard to the eschatological character of the Servant's mission, establishing *justice* in the earth, his sacrifice possesses a fullness and finality of which the cultus itself could never boast.

In applying Isa. 53:12 to himself, Jesus thus preannounced at the Supper the fullness and finality of his own sacrifice: it would be a vicarious, once-for-all sacrifice.

But now, in view of the prophecy at hand, a qualification is needed. At first blush this may sound heretical, but it cannot be helped: we must speak of a " limited " atonement. Second Isaiah defined the Servant's work as being in behalf of " us all " (v. 6) — that is, *all Israel*. True, he foresaw salvation extending through the Servant to the end of the earth (ch. 49:6). This, however, is doubtlessly to be understood as an enlarging of Israel's bounds. The Servant's universality of mission would not belittle the particular place of Israel as God's redeemed people. To the contrary, as " a light to the nations " (v. 6), the Servant would light up the way for the Gentiles' inclusion in the Israelite church. He would be numbered with the transgressors and, yes, would bear the sin of many, the sin of all.[11] But the " all " is nevertheless " us all " — all Israel, whomever that might include. Hence, the foreigners who were to be joined to the Lord would thereupon enter into Israelite worship, bringing their offerings and keeping the Sabbaths and festivals (chs. 56:6-8; 66:23) — *this*, from the most universally-minded prophet!

---

[11] " Many " in Isa. 53:12 is not exclusive (many, but not all) but inclusive (the sum total, consisting of many); this is common Semitic usage and is confirmed in v. 6, which speaks of the Servant as taking on the iniquity of " us all."

So, according to Second Isaiah, redemption is not outside Israel. One must be " in the Servant," so to speak, as now one must be " in Christ." The Servant's atoning work is operative only for those of his body. So also at the Last Supper the disciples, representing the entire new Israel, were effectually united with Jesus and made participants in his sacrifice. His sacrifice is vicarious for us, but not removed from us. It is necessarily limited in its effectiveness to those who are really involved in Jesus' obedience. For essential in his sacrifice as Servant was the establishment of God's rule among his people and their utter submission to it. It is a matter of involvement-or-else. And the good news of the upper room, taken up later in the church's preaching, is that we *are* involved!

In Terms of Effecting a New Covenant

Jesus' fulfillment of Old Testament sacrifice, as indicated in the eucharistic words, is finally to be understood in terms of effecting a new covenant: a new relationship between God and his people. I have mentioned this at points above, but it merits special consideration. We are now at the heart of the Biblical theology.

When a minister of the Sacrament says, " This is my blood of the [new] covenant," he repeats probably the most profound self-reference our Lord ever made.[12] It was easily one

---

[12] I cannot agree with those who deny that Jesus spoke of the covenant at the Supper. On the one hand, if " blood of the covenant " is deemed an impossible Aramaic construction (so J. Jeremias), the opposing view has also been argued (so G. Dalman). More importantly, even if the earliest oral (Aramaic) tradition that can be reconstructed might omit " of the covenant," such traditions were liturgical and summary in form, so that we cannot recover Jesus' *ipsissima verba*. Yet, the covenant terminology is attested in all the New Testament accounts; and the written traditions underlying those of Mark and Paul, perhaps Luke as well, were independent and very early. I therefore suppose that the meaning which Jesus intended is more reasonably to be found in such accounts designed to set it forth than in an earlier liturgical formula primarily designed for worship, which itself was probably accompanied by additional instruction. The other objection to Jesus' use of " covenant " at the Supper, on the ground that he is not reported to have used it before then, is treated below, pp. 70–72.

of his most daring self-references. If it has since lost some of its edge through hackneyed use, the saying must have first pierced Jewish ears as an almost shocking sound. In speaking of his blood of the covenant, Jesus set himself in unique relation to the entire divine purpose in history. Indeed, he claimed to be the answer to Israel's history — a history of God's covenanting which the Old Testament had left up in the air, waiting for fulfillment.

The covenant, then, in expressing the meaning of Israel's election, is both the all-embracing, unifying concept of the Old Testament and that word of God which makes it an incomplete book. There is instruction for us here.

Covenant principles in Old Testament religion. Most important to be noted about the covenant is God's primacy in it. Although the covenant was a mutual relationship between him and his people, it was basically his business. His redemption of Israel created the relationship, and his sovereign purpose kept it intact.

This primacy is attested in Israel's understanding of God and consequent understanding of herself and the world. The basic assumption of Old Testament religion is that God reveals himself as a Person with a purpose. Historically, this revelation was believed to be primarily disclosed in the exodus and the giving of the law at Sinai, where the covenant was established. Previously the nation's forebears had known God in only a limited way, but from the exodus onward he was to be known by a new name: Yahweh, the One who reveals what he is like in mighty acts (Ex. 6:3-7). In view of this new knowledge, Israel considered not only her present existence but her whole life. From God's exodus-revealed power and purpose, she looked backward to interpret her beginnings and forward to interpret what must be her good future. Both looks were cosmic in scope: the backward look ascribing creation to God in the new name, Yahweh (Gen. 2:4b ff.); the forward look anticipating a universal success of the covenant intent.

God's primacy in the covenant is also stressed by the chronology of events. Sinai is where the nation's convenantal duties are outlined — but exodus deliverance comes first. Sinai itself was understood to be the result of an extended series of events. As such it was the confirmation, not the beginning, of Israel's election. God's word to Abraham, Isaac, and Jacob had, as it were, set the Sinai event in motion long before Israel's leaders ascended the mountain for the covenant's formal inauguration.

The initiation and success of the covenant therefore lay with God. It was no mere " fifty-fifty " marriage dependent equally on each party to the union. The word "covenant" (Heb. *bᵉrīt*) need not imply an agreement between equals, but may denote a relationship especially binding on one of the partners. That such was the case between God and his people is clear enough. And the fact that he instigated the covenant, gave it stimulus in the exodus, irrevocably bound himself to it with promises — this is the only credible explanation for the certainty of Israelite hope when all semblance of hope was blown to shreds.

God's primacy in the covenant, however, was not to minimize Israel's obligations. The former rather implied the latter; for God's aim in initiating the covenant was to create a responsible people, a people to serve his redemptive purpose. That, to put it very simply, is why he entered into covenant with Israel. But two things must be underscored at this juncture.

The first concerns the intent of the law. One often hears it said that, whereas the New Testament teaches salvation by grace, the Old teaches salvation by works. The law is then supposed to be the means whereby God's people were to save themselves. Nothing could be farther from the truth! Israel's role was never to redeem herself, but to serve with thanksgiving and praise the One who had already redeemed her. His grace was a reality in the nation's life before the law was ever given — a fact said to preface the law when the covenant was made: " You have seen what I did to the Egyptians, and how I

bore you on eagles' wings and brought you to myself" (Ex.
19:4). Similarly, the covenant ritual, in its sacrifices at the foot
of Sinai and its meal eaten on the mountain in God's presence,
was the people's response to his redeeming act and the mani-
festation of their favored and real union with him.[13] In other
words, Israel's part in the covenant was to confess that redemption had freely come to her and to respond to God's grace
in grateful obedience. The law was meant to implement this,
helping the nation to mature in favor with God and man. So
even the law was a gift of grace. (Of course, we preachers
may know all this; but apparently we have failed to let num-
bers of our people in on it.)

The other emphasis needed here concerns the nature of
covenant obedience. If the Old Testament is popularly indicted
as promoting a doctrine of works salvation, it is also thought by
many to be plagued with a heavy legalism. Once again, however, the notion is sheer naïveté. Legalism was often a problem
child for the nation; but the law, from which legalistic practices derived, was not so designed originally. The obedience it
was to foster was a *living* obedience, an obedience to God's
voice (Ex. 19:5), not simply a rheumatic adherence to a fixed
set of rules. Significantly, the law was modified from time to
time, to meet altered circumstances, indicating that the concern was with obedience to God himself as his will was freshly
apprehended in changing situations.[14] It was to be a lively,
interpersonal relationship, so that Israel's faithfulness in the
covenant could never rightly be equated with an ethical for-
malism or a mechanically correct cultus. Israel had to do chiefly
not with regulations for behavior and worship but with personal God, who would regulate the nation in his active, creative word.

From this view of Israel's obligations God's covenantal purpose may be defined as the establishment of a holy govern-

[13] *Supra,* pp. 36–37.
[14] Evident in a comparison of the Book of the Covenant (Ex., chs. 20 to
23) with later enactments in the priestly law and Deuteronomy.

ment, which we call the Kingdom of God: a relationship between God and men wherein his lordship or rule is the controlling factor. Although the idea of the Kingdom awaited monarchical developments in Israelite politics before it became prominent, the basic meaning of the Kingdom can be seen as early as Sinai. There, in the covenant-making, is revealed God's aim to create a people who would relate to him as loyal subjects do to their king — a people who would be governed by their Redeemer-Lord and thereby serve his purpose. The covenant was therefore Israel's highest honor and one possibility for untold greatness.

The hope for a new covenant. The creation of such a responsible people, however, failed to be realized in ancient Israel. As the years rolled along, the covenant purpose was increasingly scandalized. The very things that confound a people's healthy relationship with the Lord — a deadly systemization of ethics, a worship devoid of concern for neighborly goodness, a desire to manipulate God, a belief that he is bound to pay respects to human selfishness — got so strong a toehold in Israel that by the eighth century B.C. hardly any hope for the present remained. And from then on, what little present hope there was finally dwindled to none. Yet, the exodus could not be forgotten, nor could the purpose of Yahweh be consigned to defeat. Those closest to his mind, therefore, saw a future realization of his rule in a " new " covenant.

Though this was the particular word of Jeremiah, the entire prophetic hope was in effect the promise of a new covenant. All that the Sinaitic covenant implied was envisioned as surely to be established in that day when God would perfectly reign over his people. But Jeremiah's formulation of this hope is no less momentous for its kinship with the general prophetic word. It ranks next to Second Isaiah's " Servant " as the summit of Old Testament prophecy and is esteemed by the gospel, in eucharistic tradition especially. Second Isaiah's genius was to announce the " how " of the new relationship: i.e., its accomplishment in the Servant's suffering. Jeremiah's genius was in his emphasis on the "what" of the new relationship: i.e., its conditions. In other words, if we may speak of forgiveness alone, Second Isaiah's peculiar stress regarded the means, Jeremiah's the results.

That Jeremiah should have been primarily interested in the "what" of the new covenant is explicable from his acute sensitivity to the nation's sin. Unequaled in Israel's history, his analysis of it revealed a complete dissolution of the people's intercourse with God, a break so irreparable that nothing could avert the onrushing doom about to crush Jerusalem. If there was to be any future hope, it had to be in terms of a new relationship utterly different from the old one, which had allowed for disastrous collapse. To this prophet, a hope that could not assure the eternal stability of Israel's restoration to God was not worth the nurture to keep it alive. Consequently, his twofold use of *bᵉrīt*, a word he employed more than any other prophet, said in effect that the old covenant had become a curse (Jer. 11:3) and that in its place would one day be an unbreakable, everlasting covenant (chs. 31:32; 50:4-5).

At this point, however, it is well to note that in Jeremiah, as in all the prophets, connection is never lost with the past. If he had to view the covenant as nullified, he did not believe God's dealings with Israel were also nullified, as though history had reached the jumping-off place. Instead, since the divine purpose will not be thwarted, but is as certain as day and night, the future true people of God were to be the seed of the patriarchs and would be ruled by one of David's descendants (ch. 33:19-26). The new Israel of the new covenant must eventually stem from the old!

The new covenant's conditions outlined in Jer. 31:31-34 speak, first, of its eternal dimension: it will be unlike the old covenant, which could be and was in fact broken. Secondly, it should have to be an inward covenant: God's law will be written on the people's hearts. Thirdly, the new relationship will be intimate and full: all God's people will "know" him. The word *yāda'* is used here to signify not mere intellectual acquaintance but the closest, personal association — as, for a similar usage, the statement that "Adam knew Eve his wife, and she conceived and bore Cane " (Gen. 4:1; cf. Jer. 2:8; 4:22; 9:3, 6). Finally, the basis of all this will be forgiveness: "*for* I will forgive their iniquity, and I will remember their sin no more" (ch. 31:34). The singular, "iniquity" and "sin," rather than the plural, expresses what the entire passage implies: namely, that what is needed, if the new covenant is to avoid the breakdown of the old, is not simply a removal of bad habits, "sins," but a fundamental change in the nature of God's people. And the great word is that just such a change will be brought about in forgiveness. It only remained for this mighty expectation to be confirmed in the Servant sacrifice of Jesus, in whom we are at once forgiven and made a new creation!

But some have doubted that Jeremiah thought of the new covenant as related to sacrifice at all. It is a view severing his hope from the past; and in that, especially, the position is indefensible. It is, of course, true that Jer. 31:31-34 has no sacrificial reference and that Jeremiah himself lambasted the practice of sacrifice (e.g., ch. 7:21-22). On the one hand, however, we should not expect any preacher to state explicitly all the theological implications of his message at a given point. On the other hand, Jeremiah's displeasure with the sacrificial worship of his day no doubt issued from the fact that Israel's sacrifices had ceased to be accompanied by faithful, covenant obedience.[15] One may no more conclude from his attacks on the cultus that Jeremiah was opposed to sacrifice per se than conclude that he was opposed to prayer per se in saying that no hope for the nation could be put in it either, regardless of who did the praying (chs. 7:16; 11:14; 14:11; 15:1)!

Yet the most striking evidence against an antisacrificial in-

---

[15] So with all the prophets in their denunciation of sacrifice. Biblical scholarship has deserted the view that the Old Testament evidences a fundamental disharmony between "prophetic" and "priestly" religion; e.g., Rowley, *op. cit.*, pp. 79–81, 88–103.

terpretation of Jeremiah's message is his expression of the future hope in terms of the cultus itself:

For thus says the LORD: . . . the Levitical priests shall never lack a man in my presence to offer burnt offerings, to burn cereal offerings, and to make sacrifices for ever. (Ch. 33:17-18.)

Rather, in the days of Israel's restoration, the Levitical priests will number like the host of the heaven and the sands of the sea (v. 22). These do not sound like the words of a man who was opposed to sacrifice itself or who meant to say that the new covenant would be established without it!

Why did Jeremiah fashion his hope that way, in terms of priests and sacrifices? Because he was no less a Hebrew than Second Isaiah or Jesus or any of the New Testament writers. The future relationship he envisioned was to be founded on forgiveness, and he could hardly conceive of that apart from what every Hebrew believed was accomplished in sacrifice. To interpret Jeremiah's new covenant nonsacrificially is to make him something he decidedly was not. And it is to confuse the way to the upper room, where Another is heard to speak of the new covenant specifically in terms of his blood.

The covenant in the New Testament generally. Turning now to the New Testament, we encounter a profound change in tense. It is no longer God *will do* such-and-so, but rather, he *has done* it. His Kingdom or rule, which is the framework of the covenant and the promise for Israel in the Old Testament, is spoken of as having arrived in Jesus (e.g., Matt. 3:1-3). He is himself the Servant-Messiah to redeem and rule God's people (v. 17).[16] The new age, with its forgiveness and wonderful works, is here: the covenant hope is fulfilled![17]

In relating to Israel's covenant theology, the New Testament

[16] The heavenly word at Jesus' baptism refers (*a*) to Ps. 2:7, relating to a king's enthronement, and (*b*) to Isa. 42:1, speaking of the Servant, and thus suggests a combining of the offices of Messiah and Suffering Servant. Note that the temptation following was that Jesus be a popular, and therefore not a suffering, Messiah (Matt 4:1-11; Luke 4:1-13).

[17] This brief statement is not to slight the tension in New Testament eschatology between the Kingdom as realized and still to come, discussed below, pp. 88-93.

writers faced no small task: how to retain the concept's fullness and keep its emphases in proper balance. The difficulty of
expressing *bᵉrīt* in another tongue is that it has a peculiar con-
notation, rooted in a particular historical revelation that is
distinct in itself. *Bᵉrīt* is but one of many words pointing up
that Old Testament Hebrew is a theological language. The
problem for translation into a nontheological or differently
orientated language is obvious. In their interpretation of the
covenant, however, the Old Testament writers and formulators of the Greek sources underlying the Gospels found help in
two ways.

One was in relying on a variety of established expressions.
Aside from the use of *bᵉrīt*, the covenant relationship is described in the Old Testament under a number of figures —
parenthood, marriage, kingship, a shepherd, a servant, and so
on. The emphases of these figures often overlap, but their
usage as a whole serves to maintain the twofold idea in *bᵉrīt:*
(1) that God is ever the initiator and primary actor in the covenant; and (2) that his people are necessarily involved and held
responsible in the covenant purpose. The intimacy of the
covenant relationship is especially suggested in the figures of
parenthood (Israel is God's own child) and marriage; the latter also implies mutual obligation (but not of equals). The
shepherd figure lays stress to the primacy of God's grace and
rule, as that of kingship emphatically points to his rule being
the framework in which the covenant exists; while the servant
figure highlights Israel's unique role in God's purpose. In taking up these figures, the New Testament preserves the wealth
of the concept and maintains the right relation between God's
covenantal primacy and his people's consequent responsibility.
Full of heart and meaning, the figures offer to enrich pulpit
and lectern, though to concentrate solely on any one of them
would result in distortion.

The other help that the New Testament's formulators found
for their interpretation of the covenant was the Septuagint's
translation of *bᵉrīt*. Two Greek words were available, *sunthēkē*
and *diathēkē*, neither of which in itself would suitably render

the meaning contained in *bᵉrît*. *Sunthēkē* (an agreement) connotes mutual responsibility well enough, but suggests a compact between peers. *Diathēkē* (a will or testament) implies God's primacy in covenanting with his people, yet suggests a one-sided responsibility in the relationship, wherein the second party is simply on a receiving end. By the time of the earliest Christian writings, however, the difficulty had been met. Through the Septuagint's reading of *diathēkē*, which the New Testament follows exclusively, this word had come to mean, for those acquainted with the Greek Old Testament, precisely what is meant in *bᵉrît*. This theological preparation of *diathēkē* for evangelistic use was an important etymological development. I daresay it related to the fullness of time. As the time was ripe for Christ's appearance, an adequate Greek word was at hand for the church's proclamation of the new covenant in him.

Besides keeping God's primacy and his people's responsibility in proper balance, the New Testament's covenant teaching also maintains the relation between old and new. Just as the prophets were concerned to say that the future new relationship would be in fulfillment of God's past covenanting with Israel, the gospel shows what has happened in Christ to be both a new thing and yet the issue of what has gone before. For instance, the author of Hebrews, referring explicitly to Jesus' sacrificial fulfillment of Jeremiah's prophecy, states that the old covenant is made obsolete by the new (Heb. 8:13); at the same time, his single concern throughout the epistle is to demonstrate that Jesus is the one, valid answer to ancient Israel's entire history and practice. So also Paul, who speaks of our being ministers of a new covenant, contrasts it with the old one (II Cor. 3:6), yet adds that in Christ the old covenant is unveiled (v. 14). This was the church's first preaching: Christ, in whom new life with God is available to men, rightly belongs to the sons of that covenant made with Israel's fathers (Acts 3:12-26).

The eucharistic reference. This vital relation between old and new got particular witness in the formulas of eucharistic worship. Mark's account of the words of institution, followed in Matthew, speaks of *the* covenant, which is obviously an allusion to the old or Sinaitic covenant. And the traditions behind Paul's and Luke's accounts speak of the *new* covenant. Since these formulas were of Palestinian origin and therefore in early coexistence, one may imagine they were conscious efforts to express together the relation of Christians to both the old and new covenants of the Hebrew Scriptures. At very least, the coexistence of these formulas reveals the church's early understanding that in Jesus the two covenants are joined and become as one.

But the most exciting evidence of this is to be found in the Synoptic reports of the Last Supper itself. Jesus is at table with his disciples, whom he selected to number as the twelve tribes of Israel. He speaks to them about the new covenant in his blood. Acting effectually for every generation of God's people, as did Israel's leaders at Sinai, the disciples then eat and drink what he offers. They and later generations are thereby united with him, receiving the gift of a new relationship with God, *and the new covenant is thus formally inaugurated.* In other words — and the similarities with Ex. 24:1-11 can scarcely go unnoticed — the Supper of the new covenant is a prophetic reenactment of the covenant-making at Sinai!

Now, what does the new covenant in Jesus' blood mean, according to the eucharistic words? The removal of sin as a barrier to fellowship! Isaiah 53:12, to which Mark (ch. 14:24) and Matthew (ch. 26:28) allude, speaks of the Servant's bearing not merely our sins but our sin. As we have noted, this same removal of sin in the singular is the emphasis of Jer. 31:34, to which Paul (I Cor. 11:25) and Luke (ch. 22:20) allude, and is indicated in Jeremiah to be the very foundation of the new covenant. In so pointing, by way of one or both of these prophecies, to the removal of sin in the singular, Jesus suggested that his sacrifice would issue in a basic conversion of the nature of God's people. Not only their sins but also their *sin* would be taken away. This is a new covenant indeed! And according to John's Gospel, this was the preaching of Jesus: "You must be born anew" (John 3:7).

God's rule, the framework of covenant, is seen in the eucharistic words to be accomplished in One whose death would be the climax of obedience. But that by itself — dare we tire of saying it? — could never have been enough. What about you and me? God's lordship or rule had to be established in the life of all his people, upon whose hearts his law would be written (Jer. 31:33). This new covenant stipulation was not to pass by the board. At the Last Supper, therefore, Jesus not only indicated that his death would mean the removal of sin as a barrier to fellowship with God, but also, as we have seen, he gave the disciples and us a share in his perfect obedience, which by virtue of our union with him would make us righteous in fact. God's covenant intent to create a truly responsible people, a purpose sunk in a history of apparent failure, would thus actually be fulfilled in Jesus' new covenant sacrifice. After centuries of nothing but a far-flung hope, a hope yonder at the end of the line, Israel's faithful prophets were about to be vindicated! Now they had only to wait for that covenant to be sealed in the cross and empowered in the resurrection.

Jesus' use of "covenant." But finally, can we ascribe this announcement to Jesus himself? It is surprising that, apart from the Synoptic and Pauline accounts of the Supper, there is no record of his ever mentioning the covenant explicitly. This is even more amazing in view of his abundant use of the Old Testament, wherein the word has central importance. One might suppose our Lord never spoke directly of the covenant. Particularly since "blood of the covenant" is at best a difficult Aramaic construction,[18] the convenantal reference in the eucharistic formulas may represent merely the church's interpretation of Jesus.

Let us first note, however, that the omission of "covenant" in the records of Jesus' speech up to the Last Supper seems not

[18] See note 12 above, where this objection is considered.

so much a negation of his alleged use of the word as its confirmation. In this case it is far easier to move forward, history-wise, than backward; far easier to move away from the Supper than back to it. For example, if Jesus did *not* mention the covenant that night, the church must have put the word on his lips to lend authority to her own interpretation (or reinterpretation?) of him. But why then did the church go no farther back with that than the upper room? This would have been a queer apology indeed! Further, why did the Gospel writers then refrain from using the word themselves, with one minor exception (Luke 1:72), in their own comments on the meaning of Jesus' life? Even aside from the fact that his reference to the covenant is certified in all four accounts of the eucharistic words,[19] a criticism that denies the authenticity of the reference, without answering such questions, is worse off than when it began. It winds up with a more difficult problem than it seeks to solve.

Nor can the situation be explained on the grounds that prior to the Last Supper, Jesus did not think much about the covenant. Although one cannot prove that he did or did not previously use the word itself,[20] there can be no doubt that he considered himself and his work covenantally. From the beginning of his public ministry, we are told, there was continually in his preaching and teaching and Messianic behavior the word about the Kingdom of God,[21] which was understood to be the framework of the covenant. In his eschatological reinterpretation of the law (e.g., Matt. 5:17-48), he claimed in effect the office of " new " Moses: that is, Giver of a new law, which implies a new covenant. In summoning not eleven or thirteen but twelve men as disciples, he prefigured the new-covenant people to be created in himself. Finally, to recall only one thing more, his consciousness of mission was bathed in the prophecy of the

[19] The shorter text of Luke's account, omitting the reference, is decidedly inferior; see Appendix A.
[20] But I find the negative position incredible in view of his abundant indications, in word and deed, of the covenantal character of his mission.
[21] *Infra*, pp. 89–91.

Servant of Yahweh, who would fulfill Israel's role as a light, that is a covenant, to the nations (cf. Isa. 49:6; 42:6). The covenant concept had flourished in Jesus' mind!

Why, then, is the word not used in the Gospels until the Last Supper? It must have resulted from something Jesus said about the covenant itself: some particular significance that it received at the Supper and had not had before. Well, we have seen that the new covenant was formally inaugurated in the upper room, where all generations of Jesus' community were sacramentally given a share in his suffering obedience and a new nature in him. I would therefore suggest that the Synoptic writers purposely reserved the word " covenant " for the record of that great hour in the church's life when, in being joined to Jesus, we were effectively constituted new Israel, the new-covenant people of God. It was a holy, memorable moment: a moment to be made all the more holy and all the more memorable by its solitary recitation of the word —this one word which, more than any other, described Israel's redeemed and responsible relationship with the Lord.

IV UNTO THE REMEMBRANCE OF JESUS

We are now to consider how the upper room event was carried into the church's sacramental practice.

Jesus sacramentally gave the disciples a part in his obedience unto death. This meant for them, as we have seen, God's gift of salvation — salvation "in union with Christ." At the Lord's Supper this gift is again offered to men, and, as at the initial celebration, they are to receive it faithfully. In grateful devotion to Christ, they are to accept it freely by eating and drinking the elements, which he causes effectually to signify that gift. In other words, what was done at the Last Supper, other than the new covenant's formal inauguration, is to be repeated over and again in the church's eucharistic worship.

THE PROBLEM

This meaning for the Sacrament receives special emphasis in Jesus' saying about "doing unto remembrance" (Luke 22:19b; I Cor. 11:24-25).[1] But even aside from that, Mark's account indicates that the Last Supper and the Lord's Supper have the same sacramental import. Without mentioning the saying, Mark assumed that the two were similar. In reporting what was said and done in the upper room, he referred to an

---

[1] The saying is most likely authentic; see Appendix B.

early liturgical formula which reflected what was said and done in eucharistic practice. Significantly, no effort was made, so far as we can tell, to add the remembrance saying to Mark's account, hoping thereby to make the connection between the Last Supper and the Lord's Supper explicit. If one asks why, the answer is unavoidable — let it be stated again: Mark and the early church as a whole apparently felt that no basic sacramental difference existed between what occurred in the upper room and what was meant to occur in eucharistic celebrations.[2]

If this were better appreciated, and if the church could dislodge herself from customary, prejudged conclusions in exegesis, we would have fewer weird and weak interpretations of the remembrance saying and of the Sacrament itself. The way must be cleared of the two most popular and extreme of these.

A sacrificing of sorts? On the one hand, what occurs in the Lord's Supper is not, in any sense, a renewal of Jesus' sacrifice; nor is it a re-presenting of him to God.[3] If it is held that Jesus' sacrifice is somehow repeated, *estin* in the bread and wine sayings must then be read substantively, which is fraught with difficulties.[4] Or if it is suggested that *poiein* (to do) in the remembrance saying means " to offer," as it occasionally does elsewhere, one need only observe that " Do this " clearly refers to the *reception* of the elements, not to their being held up before God the Father. It refers to what is signified by the worshipers' *acceptance* of the elements, as will be indicated below. Moreover, we shall see that the primary action in the Anamnesis or sacramental remembrance, like that at the Last Supper, is churchward in direction and not Godward.[5] To suppose that " Do this " means " Offer this to God " — whether

---

[2] Gregory Dix's widely known explanation of Mark's omission of the saying is considered below, in Appendix B.

[3] For this view, see Gregory Dix, *The Shape of the Liturgy,* 2d ed. (London: The Dacre Press, 1945), pp. 161, 242–247.

[4] *Supra,* p. 26.

[5] This is equally against the suggestion that the eucharistic proclamation of Christ's death, via the remembrance, is our " putting God in remembrance " of the merits of that death for us.

Christ, or a "renewed" sacrifice of him, or the believer's act of worship be the object — well, that would be a grand disregard for God's having the primary role in the Sacrament, as if to put redemption in reverse.

A human calling to mind? The other popular interpretation of the remembrance saying which must be laid aside takes it to denote merely a human remembering or calling to mind. The worshiper is simply reminded of Christ's death for him. This view, usually held in reaction to the one above, is equally inadequate. If in the former view the wrong thing is thought to be happening, in this view almost nothing is thought to be happening — except an operation of memory, accruing in whatever blessings memory might contain. Further, in this as in the former view, the sacramental remembrance action is done by men, not by God. Yet it is God, not us, to whom this action primarily belongs — a fact to be dealt with later.

The problem restated. The problem in these and various other interpretations of the saying entails a mistaking of the word "remembrance" itself (Greek, *anamnēsis*). It must get a Hebraic interpretation. That it would have at the Last Supper is certain from the entire Hebraic setting of the Supper. And that Paul could have expected even the Gentiles at Corinth so to understand his use of the word is clear from the Old Testament "quality" of I Corinthians.[6] Up to this point, therefore, we can all agree that the word requires a Hebraic interpretation. However, the Hebrew concept of remembrance, remembering, and memory admits numerous possible meanings — and the trouble comes when one of them is selected more or less arbitrarily. The question rather to ask is whether any of them particularly fits the eucharistic words themselves.

[6] Note the references to God's temple (I Cor. 3:16-17), the Passover (ch. 5:6-8), circumcision (ch. 7:18-19), details of the law (chs. 9:9; 14:21), Old Testament sacrifices (chs. 9:13; 10:18), the exodus and wilderness (ch. 10:1-10), the corporate involvement of Adam's sin (ch. 15:22), the Hebrew significance of eating and drinking (ch. 10:16-18) — all of which assumes the readers are well informed about Hebrew thought and theology.

This, then, is the issue: since Mark's use of a liturgical formula indicates that the Last Supper and the Lord's Supper share the same sacramental import, is there a Hebrew meaning of "remembrance" that suits this? More exactly, can "doing unto the remembrance of Jesus" be taken to signify in the Sacrament what also transpired in the upper room, namely, the offering to men of God's gift of salvation and their own reception of it? It can indeed.

REMEMBRANCE IN HEBREW THOUGHT: POSSIBLE MEANINGS

Hebrew references to remembrance, remembering, and memory reveal five general emphases.[7] Though one meaning shades into another, the overall usage spans a wide and diverse range. Only one of the emphases is apropos to the eucharistic words, but we have to consider each of them to see which one it is.

1. *Purely a matter of intellect.* The simplest meaning denotes purely an intellectual function. This is the sense of remembering that we most usually think of — the recollection of data. For instance, "Jerusalem remembers in the days of her affliction and bitterness all the precious things that were hers from days of old" (Lam. 1:7; cf. Isa. 43:18). Similarly, it is said that Tobit remembered Amos' prophecy and wept (Tobit 2:6-7).

2. *Incentive to certain behavior.* In the next meaning the function of intellect is still foremost, yet the intent is to motivate action or behavior. God's cursings and blessings were thus to be remembered, that Israel might return to him in obedience (Deut. 30:1-2). In Ps. 105 the exodus is recounted, so that the people, being reminded of the Lord's wondrous works, will

---

[7] Any simple arrangement of these is bound to be artificial, so complex are the usages and so divergent the meanings. Their discussion herein, in order to be a helpful introduction for most of the readers in mind, must be limited to such a general survey. One of the best studies for the serious student is that of Brevard S. Childs, *Memory and Tradition in Israel* (Alec R. Allenson, Inc., 1962).

practice reliance upon him (cf. Ps. 78:5 ff.; Isa. 44:21-22). The command in Joel 1:3, to tell succeeding generations about the devastating locusts, was for the people to heed history's lesson, lest they provoke a like judgment in the future.

Though this kind of remembering is primarily attributed to man, occasionally it is spoken of God, especially in prayerful utterances. The psalmist asks him to remember what the measure of life is and how his servant is scorned, that he might turn off the fire of his wrath (Ps. 89:46-51). Likewise God is begged to remember what has befallen Jerusalem, to behold the terrible disgrace, that he will restore his people to himself (Lam. 5:1).

3. *Certain behavior itself.* As remembering might be an incentive to certain behavior, it could also be the behavior itself. A shortcut, so to speak, was taken in expressing the thought. For instance, " Remember the Sabbath, to keep it holy " could be shortened to " Remember the Sabbath," which, of course, means to keep it holy.

Whereas in the first two meanings the intellect is the primary thing, from here on the accent is on behavior that would not be classed as essentially intellectual in character. Further, this third usage was not merely a shortcut in speech. In the one immediately above, there is always something of the subjunctive mood in the air: remembering, that such and so *might* be done. But here, especially when God is the subject, the note of uncertainty is gone. When he calls to mind, action ensues — for he is God who acts. His remembering is *doing* something about a person or situation.

Examples are many. Praying for strength, Samson asked God to remember him (Judg. 16:28). Hannah requested that he remember her, give her a son (I Sam. 1:11; cf. ch. 1:19-20). In Ps. 98:2-3, " The LORD has made known his victory " is paralleled by " He has remembered his steadfast love and faithfulness to the house of Israel." In these cases God's remembering equals his acting in favor — granting prowess, removing sterility, vindicating the faith of the elect. In other cases, notably when the whole nation is in view, his acting in compassion and mercy equals his remembering the covenant (e.g., Ps. 106:45). In contrast is the lament, with Jerusalem a wreckage, that God has forgotten his people (Lam. 5:20); for, as Hosea had said, when Israel forgets the Lord, his judgment is to forget them (Hos. 4:6).

Men also were spoken of as remembering in the sense of doing. The term often signified one's peculiar relationship with God. Remembering him was identified with fearing him (Isa. 57:11; Eccl. 12:1), not consenting to sin (Tobit 4:5), working righteousness (Isa. 64:5), and praying (Jonah 2:7). A frequent usage in this sense explicitly regarded the law, so that to remember God's name could mean to keep the law (Ps. 119:55). Or the command might simply be to remember the law (Mal. 4:4). And the Qumran sectarians, who habitually spoke of the law and covenant synonymously, liked to boast that the memory of the covenant has always been among them.[8]

4. *Bringing up to the present the effects of something done in the past.* A fourth meaning in Hebrew references to remembrance, remembering, and memory is: bringing up into the present the effects of something done in the past. This is akin to the meaning just discussed, in that both signify action that is neither simply nor primarily a process of mind. In the usage at hand, however, the emphasis is on consequences of something already done: effects that are made to be realized in a later or new situation. Also, whereas remembering in the sense of the third meaning could be attributed equally as well to either God or man, remembering in this sense was deemed the peculiar action of God. True, functions of human memory might be involved in this powerful linking of past and present: for example, a memorial or cultic recounting of an event such as the exodus, wherein the past event was "actualized" or made a contemporary, redemptive reality for the worshipers.[9]

---

[8] The War of the Sons of Light and the Sons of Darkness 13:7-8.
[9] Cf. Childs, *op. cit.*, especially pp. 66–70, 74–80.

But just as it was a really redemptive link, God's own action was basic and necessary for the human or cultic remembering to be thus effective.[10] To cause the effects of some past deed to appear freshly in the present, whether redemptively or with negative force — this presupposes sovereignty, a moral control of history, a control that is God's alone.

According to Hosea, God is he who remembers Israel's evil works, bringing judgment (Hos. 7:2). Because "Israel has forgotten his Maker" (ch. 8:14), God will remember the people's iniquities, will punish their sins, sending them back into bondage (chs. 8:13; 9:9). This making present the consequences of past sins is explicit in the law concerning marital jealousy. It stipulated an "offering of remembrance" which would "bring sin to remembrance" by issuing in bitter pain for an unfaithful wife (Num. 5:11-31). But the most dramatic example is in the widow's confrontation with Elijah. When her son became critically ill, she addressed the prophet in horror: "What have you against me, O man of God? You have come to me to bring my sin to remembrance, and to cause the death of my son!" (I Kings 17:18).

When God remembers sins, therefore, it is his setting judgment into sure and speedy motion. So was he asked, in a spirit of revenge, to remember against the Edomites (Ps. 137:7) and, later, to remember the lawless destruction (II Macc. 8:4). So also had Jeremiah declared that God was about to remember the people's iniquities (Jer. 14:10); and once the judgment arrived, leaving the land a desolation, the explanation was simply that the Lord had remembered (ch. 44:21). Since he is in control, the historically informed among his people earnestly pray for mercy, asking that he not remember the sins of their forefathers (Baruch 3:5; cf. Ps. 79:8)! It was not a prayer

---

[10] Cf. *ibid.*, pp. 83–89. Childs rightly urges that the dynamic connection via tradition (i.e., via Israel's memory) between present time and historically fixed events of the past must be understood in the sense that history, by God's own action, is made to be redemptive history: his redemptive action in past and unrepeatable events is not static but rather continues.

for a cosmic case of amnesia!

As past sins are thus remembered by God, so are deeds of righteousness. This is voiced in Jeremiah's prayer for vindication (Jer. 15:15) and Nehemiah's repeated request that he and his faithfulness be remembered (Neh. 5:19; 13:14, 22, 31; cf. chs. 6:14; 13:29). So too the prayer that God remember in David's favor for his having intended to build a dwelling place for the Lord (Ps. 132:1-5), and the general petition that God remember those who have willingly revered him (II Esdras 8:28).

Not only past deeds of men but also past deeds of God were spoken of as effectively remembered by him. The psalmist's plea, "Remember thy word to thy servant, in which thou hast made me hope" (Ps. 119:49), is obviously a request for God to cause the word he *has* spoken to become powerfully effective here and now. More often, however, this remembering is related to the covenant made long ago — e.g., the introductory blessing in II Macc. 1:2-3, that God bless the people and remember his covenant with Abraham, Isaac, and Jacob.

5. *Signifying existence.* The last usage to be noted here signifies existence. It was actually a mingling of ontological emphases, some of which are occasionally implied in the above usage of God's remembering or bringing to remembrance something out of the past. But the emphasis on existence was often singular and therefore earns separate mention.

It might be, first of all, on the existence of lasting effects. For example, it is said that the righteous man will be remembered forever (Ps. 112:6), in that his righteousness endures forever (v. 9), which is contrasted with the wicked man's desire coming to naught (v. 10). In other words, the *effects* of the righteous will continue forever. This meaning is related to that which emphasizes *effective* existence or simply the *fact* of existence. To cite another example, God's enemies would like to destroy the strength of his people, rooting out their memory from the place (I Macc. 3:35). They are enemies who say, "Come, let us wipe them out as a nation; let the name of

Israel be remembered no more! " (Ps. 83:4).

In reality, however, the destroying or preserving of one's remembrance can properly be ascribed only to God. Despite the intent of his enemies, he alone is in moral control. The power is uniquely his, for example, to "blot out the remembrance of Amalek from under heaven" (Ex. 17:14), and again, in contrast to making the nation increase, to visit the wicked with destruction and erase all remembrance of them (Isa. 26:14-15). So was it prophesied of the Day of the Lord, when he would create new heavens and a new earth, that the former things would not be remembered (ch. 65:17); that is, they simply would not *be*. The same is said of the new age in II Baruch 44:9, that there will be no remembrance of the present time, which is defiled with evils. In this sense, then, remembrance signifies existence, and no remembrance means no existence or at least no effective existence.

THE REPEATED RECEPTION OF GOD'S GIFT

Now, which of these Hebrew meanings specially fits the eucharistic words? Plainly, the fourth meaning, i.e., God's bringing up into the present the effects of something done in the past.[11]

When it is said that the church celebrates the Sacrament *unto the remembrance of Jesus*, it means emphatically that God thereby ushers into the present the effects of Jesus' past and

---

[11] So Dix, *loc. cit.* Yet, he sees in the remembrance not only the effects of Christ's past deed but also the deed itself as brought up into the present or re-presented in a sense of being continued; but as Childs (*ibid.*) stresses, Hebrew thought in this regard did not imply a recurrence or continuation of past deeds themselves, rather a new and lively encounter with their redemptive reality in terms of God's ongoing activity. Further, in Dix's view, the re-presenting is an offering done by the celebrants. This would fortify the position that the Sacrament is a sacrifice of sorts; but it is undercut by the fact that, in this particular Hebrew usage of "remembrance," the primary action belongs to God. The eucharistic remembrance, we will see, is not an offering Godward but an offer churchward.

completed sacrifice. The effects of his obedience unto death are made a present reality. That is to say, salvation in Christ is made a present reality. This is precisely what was given to the disciples in the upper room: salvation in Christ as a gift received in faith. In this interpretation of *anamnēsis*, the continuity between the Last Supper and the Lord's Supper is therefore maintained and stressed.

This is not to suggest that eucharistic observance somehow makes us " more saved " or " more united " with Christ, as though we did not already corporately share with him his life, death, and resurrection. Rather, it is to recognize that, in our fellowship with him, we are in *process* of being saved. That is what salvation is — not a point-blank accomplishment merely, but a linear relationship. Hence the three main tenses of *sōzein* (to save) in the New Testament: past, present, and future. To wit: " I have been saved, I am being saved, I will be saved." And what the Sacrament of the Lord's Supper holds for us is God's salvation coming to us repeatedly: his re-creating, life-giving gift being repeatedly offered and repeatedly received.

According to the Marcan eucharistic formulation, as we have seen, the meaning of Jesus as One who was broken in obedience unto death, signified in the broken bread and outpoured wine, is offered for men to take freely and faithfully. To take it so is to receive the gift of what Jesus himself means. The remembrance motif in the Pauline and Lucan formulations does not add anything to that, it only makes it more emphatic. Namely, in the church's faithful eucharistic practice Jesus is brought to remembrance by God the Father, who causes the effects of his sacrificial deed in the past to be present and effectual for faith here and now. That is what it means to " Do this *eis tēn emēn anamnēsin* " — to receive the gift! And it is noteworthy that *emēn* in this phrase is objective.[12] The remem-

---

[12] " The use of the objective genitive with *anamnēsis* is firmly established. . . ." Joachim Jeremias, *The Eucharistic Words of Jesus*, tr. by Arnold Ehrhardt (The Macmillan Company, 1955), p. 162n6.

brance is not "*my* remembrance" but "the remembrance of
me" — i.e., God's bringing up to the present the effects of sacrificial Jesus himself, which accords exactly with our reading
"body" in the bread saying to denote the sacrifice of Jesus'
whole person.[13]

That this sacramental import was understood as intended for
the church's eucharistic worship is further evidenced in Paul's
own commentary about "doing unto the remembrance of Jesus." It comes right on the heels of the remembrance saying,
thus: "*For* as often as you eat this bread and drink the cup,
you proclaim the Lord's death until he comes" (I Cor. 11:26).
Note the fact carefully: it is the eating and drinking through
which God works the remembrance. Salvation issuing out of a
past event is made a present reality for the church *in the
church's acceptance of it*. And we are reminded that Hebrews
believed that divine gifts could be imparted through faithful
eating and drinking! The church acts in faith, sacramentally
receives with open and empty hands God's gift in Christ, and
thereby "proclaims" his death. Her preaching in the Sacrament is a preaching of Christ crucified, yet a preaching she
does almost in silence, as it were. At the Lord's Table we proclaim the redemptive meaning of his death by faithfully taking
its effects as presently our own. And is it not true that some of
the best preaching God's people do is simply in their being
visible recipients of his mercy?

I would not disparage the foremost importance of that
preaching which must be attempted from the pulpit. Not for a
moment! The plain, and sometimes painful, fact is that this
sacramental preaching is not apt to be grasped or appreciated
until the pulpit itself is given more serious attention by ministers and parishioners alike. Moreover, the preaching of the pulpit and that of the Table are both meant to be "unto the remembrance of Jesus." Each is meant to issue here and now in
a faithful reception of the effects of his one-time obedience
unto death. That is a faithful reception of salvation itself —

[13] *Supra*, pp. 16–22.

the re-creating forgiveness, the life-giving gift that we need to receive again and again and again.

THE PRIMARY ACTOR IN THE SACRAMENT

Now, obviously, this is all a rather "high" view of the Lord's Supper. Someone may therefore be asking, sardonically or seriously, whether eucharistic observance is then necessary for salvation. The answer is an unqualified *No!* The New Testament nowhere levies such a requirement.[14] The Old Testament taught a necessary sacramentalism, yes, but only with a view to the necessity of sacrifice for atonement. But the New Testament teaching is that all such sacrifice has been fulfilled and ended in the once-for-all sacrifice of Christ.

Still, the question has been forced on us from two directions. On the one hand, it comes from a people who, consumed with programs and administrative busyness, have grown (?) to depreciate the vitality of corporate worship — a people whose own Christian vitality must then be soberly questioned. Ecclesiastical organization has become increasingly and unavoidably complex. This is a complex society in which the church must try to witness, and she needs finely developed machinery for it. But it is nonetheless pathetic that committees are often held to be more meaningful than communion.

How different the church's mood at her birth! When Jesus spoke of the disciples' future "doing unto the remembrance of him," he assumed that they would continue to meet and dine together as his special friends. Hence, particularly, Paul's formulation of the remembrance saying in connection with the wine's distribution: "Do this, *hosakis ean pinēte* [i.e., as often

---

[14] Not excluding the remembrance saying, with its imperative "Do this," which is often incorrectly termed a "command to repeat" the rite. As I indicate below in regard to Paul's formulation of the saying in connection with the wine's reception, Jesus assumed the disciples would continue to meet as a table fellowship in his name. The imperative, rather than commanding a repetition of the rite, relates to the meaning or intent of the rite itself.

as you might ever be drinking], in remembrance of me" (I Cor. 11:25). According to this, the disciples were not commanded to keep on eating and drinking together. That they would do anyway. Rather, they were told to do it specifically unto the remembrance of Jesus. The command deals not with a needful repetition of the rite, but with its meaning or intent. Here was a group of men who, Jesus knew, would be made keenly aware of their vital oneness and common need: a group which, upon his resurrection, would just naturally continue to assemble as a table fellowship in his name. At such times they should receive the bread and wine " unto the remembrance of him." The question of a necessary Eucharist apparently never entered their minds. They would not approach the Table to do something they absolutely had to do there, as if God's saving forgiveness were to be offered them at no other place. Nevertheless, they would be drawn to the Table time and again, to receive the gift in faith. It was not necessary to go to the Table. But who could keep them away?

On the other hand, the question of necessary eucharistic participation comes from a segment of the church which at times has seemed to believe that she controls the Sacrament. Just how far this idea has been from even the necessary sacramentalism of the old covenant is clear when we recall that the primary Actor in Israel's sacrificial worship was rightly understood to be God. So, for example, the reason advanced against consuming blood: " For the life of the flesh is in the blood; and *I have given it* for you *upon the altar* to make atonement for your souls " (Lev. 17:11). That is to say, God himself gave the sacrifice. Not only did he participate with his people in their sacrificial worship, he was the Prime Mover in it. The sacrifices ordained for Israel's welfare were solely controlled by him. And when the nation forgot the fact, the prophets came center stage with their thundering denouncements of the business. Moreover, the effectiveness of sacrifice depended neither wholly nor primarily upon the sincerity of those making it, as if Old Testament theology were one of salvation by obedience and humble confession. That would still constitute an *opus operatum*, which is near to the heart of paganism. Instead, he who controls the movement and meaning of history no less controls the benefits that accrue to men in their worship of him. When the Hebrew sacrificed aright, whatever good effects that came to him were purposely sent by the Lord.

So too is he Primary Actor in the church's eucharistic worship. The particular kind of remembrance that the Lord's Supper involves is, according to Hebrew usage and as we have seen, properly attributed only to God. Although the Sacrament stimulates human memory, as did the cultic memorial in Israelite worship,[15] nonetheless it is *God* who works the remembrance, making the effects of Jesus' past deed actually present for faith. *He* sacramentally offers to men the gift of salvation, *he* controls the effectiveness of its representation in the prophetically symbolic action of defining and distributing the elements, *he* makes our participation in and with Christ a reality for us. And *he* judges those who would dare consume the bread and wine apart from repentance and obedient faith.

Then what is the *church's* eucharistic role? Simply to receive the gift! Not to make it operative, not to enhance its effectiveness, not to conjure up a fleeting sense of Christ's closeness for the unfortunate man whose ulcerated stomach or other condition will not normally allow him a " spiritual experience." But to receive the gift in faith, at the Table and anywhere else God graciously offers it to us.

This primary action in the Lord's Supper, coming as it does " from above," reminds us how utterly humble our real condition is. Just as the present tense of *sōzein* in the New Testa-

[15] Incidentally, " memorial " can be a legitimate term for the Lord's Supper, *if* it is taken Hebraically to denote a worshipful recounting of a past event wherein the redemptive effects from the event are brought up into the present situation by virtue of God's own continuing action; see especially notes 9 and 10. When using the term eucharistically, however, most Protestants have meant a memorial simply in the sense of a commemoration and reminder to the human mind and spirit — something more like a statue and inscription than a lively encounter with God's redemptive activity.

ment tells that redemption is necessarily a present activity of God, as well as a past and future one, the Sacrament affirms what a dependent people we are at all times. Therein we are offered, repeatedly, the one thing we always need: not merely "spiritual strength" or "food for the soul" but *salvation* in the forgiveness of sins!

It is the gift of him who is love, whose nature is therefore to give, and whose purpose is to keep on saving his people.

V THE KINGDOM AND MESSIANIC FEASTING

We must say a final word about the eschatological character of eucharistic worship. This may be done most profitably in terms of Messianic feasting. The theme of Messianic feasting has been slighted in eucharistic observance, probably since its meaning has yet to receive in Biblical studies generally the attention it deserves. A prominent figure in the Gospels, it should certainly be a resonant note in the church's celebration of the Supper of him who is called the Christ. The *Lord's* Supper is the *Messiah's* Supper.

THE TENSION IN NEW TESTAMENT ESCHATOLOGY

In that it betrays a tension between the now that is and the future that will someday be, Messianic feasting is representative of Christian eschatology as a whole. The New Testament speaks of the *eschaton,* the end-time or new age, as both a present reality and something still ahead. The Kingdom of God, his Lordship or rule, had long been promised to be established with the Messiah's arrival. And the announcement in Jesus is that the Kingdom's coming is a fact to behold in him, yet a thing for which Christians should pray.

Unless exegesis takes an arbitrary turn, this tension between "realized" and "futurist" eschatology must be honored. If the evidence were fairly one-sided, a procedure that reads one of the tenses literally and the other figuratively might be justified. But the evidence is not one-sided. Moreover, an arbitrary interpretation bent on removing the tension only makes the dilemma worse. If the Kingdom is merely future, God's rule was not really established in Jesus, and Jesus was far less Messiah than the prophets had expected. But if the Kingdom is merely present, history lacks ultimate meaning and the prophetic hope outran God's purpose. On both exegetical and theological grounds, therefore, the tension had best be kept.

Realized eschatology. By "realized" eschatology we mean that the Kingdom of God in the new age is here. There are actually two facets of this in the New Testament. In one sense, the new age cannot be said to have come until Jesus' earthly ministry was complete, with everything done that had to be done for atonement to be accomplished. It was the divine imperative for him: he *must* go to Jerusalem (Matt. 16:21), where his obedience would be filled up and God would undo sin and death through him. In another sense, the new age was present throughout Jesus' ministry, in that God's Kingdom or rule was operating toward perfection in him, day to day, hour to hour. The hard reality of it, struggling for complete domination in him, is what was moving him on to the city.

The evidence for a realized eschatology is seen, first, in Jesus' preaching and teaching. His ministry began with the word, "the kingdom of God is at hand" (Mark 1:15), is present; [1] and his lessons for Israel could be received only with this word in mind. For example, his relationship to the law. He declared it would be fulfilled in himself (Matt. 5:17), and claimed authority over it: "You have heard that it was said . . . but *I* say to you . . ." (vs. 21 ff.). His reinterpretation of the law assumes a radically new situation. This is especially clear in his handling of the divorce question. The old teaching

[1] Not "is near and about to come" but "has arrived" — the same word the Twelve (Matt. 10:7) and/or Seventy (Luke 10:9) were told to preach and to accompany with powerful works that would demonstrate the new age's arrival.

(Deut. 24:1-4), permitting divorce, was a necessary compromise of God's will; but now his will is fully disclosed, and divorce is no longer excusable on any ground (Mark 10:2-12).[2] This is to say the new age has arrived, bringing with it power for a higher righteousness!

Let us not dodge the implications for our own Christian ethics. Namely, we ought to be more righteous than old Israel ever was or could be! Granted, Jesus' reinterpretation of the law is to drive us into reliance on him, in whom alone can we be justified. Yet, just as we are united with him is there a new power at our disposal. Hence, the Sermon on the Mount is a twofold, integrated, and proper preaching: it proclaims Christ's fulfillment of all God's demands for us and the greater-than-ever responsibility that is ours.

The reality of the Messianic age got further publication in Jesus' performing the works of that age — healing the sick, cleansing lepers, casting out demons, restoring sight to the blind, raising the dead, preaching good news to the poor (Luke 7:18-22). These things, the prophets had said, were to signify the appearance of end-time salvation — and here was One doing them in abundance! Likewise, in dining with publicans and sinners he prophetically enacted the word that the eschatological redemption of the nations was being solidified in himself.[3] But his most electrifying, awesome dramatization of the new age's arrival was in what we have seen of his entry into Jerusalem at Passover season, when he came as Messiah on a beast of burden and immediately identified himself with the Temple

[2] The exception on grounds of unchastity (Matt. 5:32; 19:9) is against not only Mark but Luke (ch. 16:18) and Paul (I Cor. 7:10-11) as well; it is out of place in Matt., ch. 5, where Jesus' other reinterpretations are all stricter than any rabbinic teaching (yet the school of R. Shammai also justified divorce only in cases of adultery); and it slights the Biblical view (reflected in Matt. 19:3-8 itself!) that man and wife, serving the *imago Dei*, are to mirror the social nature of God, who loves and does for us in spite of our unfaithfulness to him. For these and other reasons, critical scholarship regards the exception as certainly alien to Jesus' teaching.

[3] *Infra*, pp. 100–101.

(Mark 11:7-11): God's rule was being established in him whose way of being King was to be a sacrifice.[4]

Following his resurrection and ascension, Jesus' message of "the Kingdom of God at hand" was taken up in the preaching and life of the church. *He has risen!* To accept this alone was to be a "realized eschatologist," proclaiming in word and deed that the future is here. The outpouring of the Spirit (Acts 2:1-4), fulfilling Joel's new-age prophecy (Joel 2:28-29), sent the word on its way. It was at the core of the earliest Christian preaching (Acts, chs. 2 to 11) and continually served as the key to the past, the secret of present power, and an assurance of things to come.

What a breathtaking word it was! According to the author of Hebrews, the law had but a shadow of this time's realities (Heb. 10:1), whereas Christ's superiority and finality are attested in his eternal priesthood (ch. 7), his once-for-all sacrifice (ch. 10:11-14), and his mediating a new covenant that makes the old one obsolete (ch. 8:6-13). The prophets are therefore fulfilled (I Peter 1:10-12); so too the law, which is even terminated in Christ (Rom. 10:4). In him God has done what the law could not — released men from sin and death (ch. 8:2-3). Through this one Man history has been converted, for now it is righteousness, not sin, which reigns in human life (ch. 5:15-21). The Christian's lot is fully sufficient, he is enabled in Christ to take whatever comes along (Phil. 4:11-13). The principalities have been plundered, and we, being delivered from the dominion of darkness, are transferred to the Kingdom of God's Son (Col. 1:13; 2:15). Since that Kingdom cannot be shaken, now is the time for thanksgiving (Heb. 12:28).

Futurist eschatology. The newness and vitality of this age notwithstanding, it was also clear to the early church that "the end is not yet." What has already come is nothing short of astounding — but still more is to come! Parousia is still to come! The hope took a root in no pagan immortality-of-the-soul concept, which colors much of today's Christianity and rids

[4] *Supra,* p. 15.

both the individual and history of the need of God. It rather looked for an all-embracing act of God himself. What A. M. Hunter has said of Paul applies to every New Testament writer:

He thought cosmically, not merely in terms of individuals. He believed not simply in an after life but in a final " wind up " of human history, the coming of Christ in glory, the Resurrection, the Last Judgment.[5]

New Testament faith is both confidently contained and restless, able for the present and yet dissatisfied with it. Having tasted and seen that God's rule is good, it hungers for more of the same. So it lives in persistent anticipation of the end. From Luke's record of the ascension (Acts 1:9-11) to John's last word in Revelation, one sees a church with her eyes fixed on heaven and on her lips the prayer, " Come, Lord Jesus! "

In this hope suffering was endured and holiness motivated (I Peter 1:6 ff.). Faith and faithfulness went hand in hand, the one abetting the other. True, the church first supposed the end would come shortly — a supposition destined to meet disappointment. But the hope would not die for that. The end would come nonetheless, maybe before this sentence is finished. . . . Well, it is still about to come! And when it does and Christ appears, " we shall be like him, for we shall see him as he is " (I John 3:2). Then will all creation " confess that Jesus Christ is Lord, to the glory of God the Father " (Phil. 2:11). Surely, what was begun in Christ will be brought to completion (ch. 1:6). And the entire cosmos will be in subjection to God the Father, for Christ will have destroyed every rule, authority, and power (I Cor. 15:24-27).

Where did this futurist eschatology find support? In the demonstrated certainty of God's purpose, of course. Things were not exactly as the prophets had envisioned them! Sin, though ultimately doomed, continues to exist; and Christians, though not ultimately bound by it, continue to sin day by day.

[5] Archibald M. Hunter, " The Hope of Glory," *Interpretation*, 8:131-132 (April, 1954).

Something should be done about that, and something would be done. It was a hope well nourished. No mere abstraction, faith's positiveness about it fed on God's decisive act in the cross and resurrection.

However, we must not err in thinking this futurist eschatology was simply dictated by necessity. It was not something the church created in face of a less-than-ideal situation, any more than the prophets' hope, spoken in bad times, was merely a logical deduction of their belief in God. In both Testaments hope is the direct issue of God's own word. It is credible because *he* has spoken it. He creates it, which alone accounts for its almost unbelievable tone and tenacity. So here, the church's forward-looking hope is an inheritance bequeathed by Jesus. He was a "futurist eschatologist" himself, not just a "realized" one.[6] This will be evident as we consider his eschatological teaching in terms of Messianic feasting.

Messianic Feasting as an Expression of Hope

Messianic feasting was one of the most popular, exciting figures of the time. Containing the promise of God's Messiah, it yearned for the day that he would come to restore Israel's fortunes and feed his people in plenty. That would be a blessed day, a great and happy day, when the Messianic feasting began, heralding the redemption of Zion. The righteous could only await it, but in the meantime the figure would be something to cherish. It therefore prospers in Jewish literature of the intertestamental and New Testament periods,[7] as well as in the Gospels.

What is noticeable about all this, however, is that nowhere is the meaning of the figure explained. Whatever significance it had was taken for granted — a fact witnessing to the vivid-

[6] Albert Schweitzer's famed position, viewing Jesus as a "mistaken eschatologist" who equated Parousia with his own resurrection, has been soundly discredited on critical grounds: e.g., John Wick Bowman, "'The Quest of the Historical Jesus,'" *Interpretation*, 3:184-193 (April, 1949).
[7] Cf. I Enoch 48:1; 62:14; II Baruch 29:3-8; Pirque Aboth 3:20; *et al.*

ness of the concept in the minds of Jesus' contemporaries. It did not *need* explanation.

Now it is apparent right off that the reference is to an eschatological feast of redemption; and that, in fact, is the heart of it. But what are its assumptions? its definite emphases? and how came such things to be? There is a store of wealth to be found in the figure when the answers to these questions are sought. We therefore return to the Old Testament, out of which grew both the Jewish and Christian literature of the day, for the foundations of the concept of Messianic feasting.

The Old Testament rootage. With regard to those foundations, there is to be seen in the Old Testament not the full flower but rather the seed of the figure that later flourished. Clear-cut references to a specifically Messianic feasting are wanting, the only exceptions being Micah 5:2-4; Zech. 9:17; and Ezek. 34:23-24. Likewise, explicitly eschatological references, in comparison to the later appearances, are also fewer than one might expect. The reason, of course, is that Israel's eschatological hope was a gradual development, directly proportionate to the waning of hope for the present. As there came to be less and less confidence in human resources for a proper relation to God, the nation's hope for the future intensified and lengthened. Hence, what had been said about God's feeding his people, which originally may have meant a present or near-present action, was extended into the end-time.

Turning to particular texts, it is to be remembered that God's providing sustenance for his people is not merely a future something. It is what he *has done* for them; and so long as food is being provided, it is what he *continues to do* for them. The hope of Messianic or eschatological feasting sprang not from dry ground, but was the product of Israel's doctrine of God: namely, that he gives and sustains all life and brings his purpose to sure fruition.

Some of the Old Testament's most sumptuous words were thus delivered, with a hungry people in view. Amos, who was sent to prophesy ruinous judgment against a morally degener-

ate nation, nevertheless expected days when God would re-
build Israel's cities and make the land exceedingly fruitful
(Amos 9:13-15). Second Isaiah's many references to future
feeding are likewise to be understood, in contrast to a wrecked
and pillaged land: the people themselves, not some invading
foreigner, will eat what they plant (Isa. 62:8-9; 65:21-22). This
was the setting of all of the prophets' hopeful words about future feedings: a present or soon-to-be-realized want of physical
food.

According to every such promise, it is God's people alone
who will be fed. This, however, means not simply the narrow
nation as it was. It ultimately means the great nation as it
would come to be. The Israel bowed down under judgment
would be released and given unfailing bread (ch. 51:14). Yet,
especially as Second Isaiah saw it, redemption would eventually embrace the other nations as well in a "new" Israel.
Everyone is invited to come, "buy wine and milk without
money and without price" (ch. 55:1). Similarly, the author of
the Isaianic apocalypse pictured a feast on the mountain for
all peoples (ch. 25:6). This inclusion of the nations in God's
one people, with free food dispensed to all, would be the consummation of his purpose in covenanting with old Israel originally (ch. 55:3-5).

Further, wherever the announcement of eschatological feeding appears, the realization of Israel's covenant obligations is
either expressed or implied. Joel, for example, spoke of the
time when Zion's sons would "eat in plenty and be satisfied"
(Joel 2:26) and God would pour out his spirit on all flesh (v.
28). In other words, God himself will then control his people;
their behavior will come under his direct influence, his *rûaḥ*.
And Second Isaiah set the future feasting in a context of
(1) obedience — "Hearken diligently to me, and eat what is
good" (Isa. 55:2); and (2) a new creation — the Lord will
fashion new heavens, a new earth, a rejoicing Jerusalem, and a
people in whom he will be glad; and never again will another
take away their food (ch. 65:17-22). Here, then, in the figure

of feedings to come, is the promise of a righteous Israel: a
people to delight the Lord, who himself will make them so.
Redemption is thus to issue in more, not less, responsibility. A
word for the church perhaps?

As for the three Old Testament references to a specifically
Messianic feasting, they have significantly in common an emphasis on humility. Ezekiel, anticipating a time when God
would feed his sheep in justice (ch. 34:13-16), said this would
be done through David (v. 23). But not David the splendid
king who leads a mighty army. Rather, David the shepherd
prince, whose single concern to feed God's sheep is opposed
to the selfish concern of Israel's false shepherds. A shepherd's
lot requires noble humility, in that his one consuming interest
must be the welfare of his flock. But hear this: " Ho, shepherds
of Israel who have been feeding yourselves! " (v. 2.) No other
description could so forcibly point the infamy of a leadership
that had failed by default. Placed against this self-seeking in-
difference is the most sensitive word ever given a prophet to
speak:

> I will save my flock, they shall no longer be a prey; and I will
> judge between sheep and sheep. And I will set up over them one
> shepherd, my servant David, and he shall feed them: he shall feed
> them and be their shepherd. And I, the LORD, will be their God,
> and my servant David shall be prince among them; I, the LORD,
> have spoken. (Vs. 22-24.)

So the Messiah to preside at the future feeding will be humble,
a servant shepherd.

Ezekiel's presentation of this word was bracketed by those
of Micah and Zechariah. In the earlier prophecy of Micah, the
humility of the Messiah's sustaining rule is emphasized in
the announcement that he will come, to " feed his flock in the
strength of the LORD " (Micah 5:4), from little Bethlehem
Ephrathah (v. 2) — hence, a shepherd who hails from a tiny
place. In the later prophecy of Zechariah it is expressed in the
figure of the Messiah riding a lowly beast of burden (Zech.
9:9). Although the prophet of chs. 9 to 14 does not say that the

people will be fed directly by the Messiah, he does say grain and wine will be provided on the day of his arrival (ch. 9:17). That this was taken to mean Messianic feasting is certain, as it is a feasting in the Messianic age of salvation. The especially important note here, however, is its being feasting in the age of a Messiah who is described as " triumphant and victorious," yet "humble" (v. 9).

Therefore — and it is a notable fact for study of the New Testament against its environment [8] — the only three Old Testament references to a specifically Messianic feasting share in common the related New Testament emphasis on humility, an emphasis to be seen at the Last Supper particularly.

The basic substructure. In answer to what underlay the Old Testament's words about future or Messianic feasting, beliefs in at least three related areas must be taken into account.

One area is what we have seen of the significance of eating and drinking: (1) to have an abundant or even adequate food and water supply was a sign of God's favor; (2) communion with him could be actually effected, and divine gifts be actually imparted, through eating and drinking; (3) God was considered Primary Actor in this effecting of fellowship and imparting of gifts; and (4) to eat and drink *in faith*, which was necessary to receive such benefits, was to manifest one's own obedient response to God's saving grace. Whatever else the future feeding means, therefore, it signifies that benefits of God's favor are to be received in faithful, covenant fellowship with him and that he will see to it himself.

A second belief to note in the substructure of Messianic feasting is the conception of man as a psychophysical being. It will be remembered that the Hebrew viewed man not as a complex of essentially heterogeneous parts but as a totality: "an animated body, and not an incarnated soul." It follows

---

[8] The New Testament teaching goes directly back to the Old Testament for its expression, largely bypassing contemporary Judaism — further indication Jesus felt his real kinship was with the Old Testament itself rather than with contemporary " extensions " of it.

from this view that food and drink are necessary not only for man's life here and now. Being what he is, he cannot have any life, anywhere or anytime, without them. This, at least, is how the ancient Hebrew looked at life.

This leads to the third belief lying at the base of Messianic feasting: the belief that God alone gives and sustains all life. If there is to be a life after death or a life for the nation in a new age, the food and drink necessary for that life will therefore have to be provided by him.

The Isaianic apocalypse holds singular interest at this point. Although the idea of "eternal" life is all but totally absent elsewhere in the Old Testament,[9] the author or editor of Isa., chs. 24 to 27, links God's swallowing up death forever with his preparing a feast for all peoples (ch. 25:6-8). That this reflects the Hebrew psychology and significance of eating and drinking seems hardly questionable: eternal life requires a resurrection body (ch. 26:19) and therefore physical sustenance to keep that body going. In other words, according to the ancient Hebrew view, the life-giving salvation that God will provide is not to be apart from eating and drinking, through which divine gifts are often imparted.

The meaning. From this survey of the Old Testament witness, we can now state directly and more fully the meaning of Messianic feasting, as it derived from Israel's Scriptures and was to find an outlet in Christ.

1. The references in both Old and New Testaments are obviously to be understood within the context of salvation. As an expression of eschatological hope, the figure points to the realization of God's purpose in a new age. This came to be interpreted as the age of the Messiah, who would be sent to usher it in, delivering his people from whatever enslaved them, ministering to their needs, and securing God's rule over all.

2. The life of God's people in the Messianic age is signified

[9] Elsewhere explicit only in Dan. 12:2, though implied or anticipated in Job 19:26 and some of the psalms (Ps. 49:15; 73:24; perhaps Ps. 16:10-11 and 17:15).

to be that of a redeemed people dwelling in full fellowship with him. It will be a covenantal fellowship, with all that that implies. Indeed, those who dine together at the humble Messiah's Table will thereby be intimately bound to him and to one another. They will be God's good people in fact, for as the obedient sheep of his pasture they will thrive under the Messiah's shepherding care.

3. The vitality of the redeemed in their fellowship with God will thus be marked by complete dependence on him. The figure of feasting to come is unsurpassed in the Old Testament in its emphasis on the dependent nature of the future life. It tells of One whose habit is to give, and of a people whose primary business will be to receive in obedience and thanksgiving the unmerited benefits he offers them.

This dependency in the future life is further stressed by the Messianic feasting's being a continual thing. The figure is usually referred to nowadays as the Messianic Banquet, the Heavenly Feast, or the Feast of the Kingdom of God. But such terms are less than adequate. They suggest a single meal with a definite ending. Yet, all the Biblical references, excepting the one in Isa. 25:6 to the feast on the mountain and the one in Rev. 19:9 to the marriage supper of the Lamb — all the others express or imply continual feasting.[10] It is likely implied in Jesus' reference to those who "will sit at table" in the Kingdom of God (Matt. 8:11; Luke 13:29). It is even clearer in the statement, "That you may *be eating* and *be drinking* at my table in my kingdom" (Luke 22:30). These verbs (*esthēte* and *pinēte*) are present subjunctive, stressing progressiveness of action, rather than the more frequently used aorist subjunctive.

Whether he considered it literally or figuratively, Jesus would naturally think of the future feasting as continual. Messianic

10 Excluding references to the feast of judgment, which *is* depicted as a single meal. Also, the single-meal references of Matt. 22:1-14; 25:1-13, and Luke 12:36 speak not of Kingdom-feasting but of a marriage feast illustrating truths about the Kingdom's nature; so too the banquet figure in Luke 14:16-24.

feasting signified redemption dependent on God; eternal life means life dependent on God. Jesus would not view such dependency as ending an hour or a week or a millennium after the onset of Parousia! To the contrary, the Messiah's appearance to feed his people would be just the beginning of their full recognition of dependence. Insofar as it represents our receiving the benefits of God's fellowship, Messianic feasting must be eternal feasting — as eternal as the life we have in the resurrected body of Christ.

Let it be stated again, with respect to precision in speech. The men of ancient Israel, though they often failed to practice it, believed that all of life is utterly subject to God's creative and sustaining activity. The New Testament church concurred. Whatever may legitimately be said to remind us of this dependence should be said. Hence, " the Messianic Feasting " is to be preferred to such single-meal terms as " the Messianic Feast " or " Banquet " — just because what it emphasizes is true.

MESSIANIC FEASTING IN JESUS' MINISTRY

Jesus' public application of Messianic feasting was many-sided. He employed it to announce his Messiahship, to declare the universality of God's purpose in himself, occasionally to refute the religionists who opposed him. More often than not, it got him in trouble. But he made it a mighty, twofold proclamation about " the Kingdom at hand " and " the Kingdom to come."

Indicating a realized eschatology. His use of the figure to indicate a realized eschatology is demonstrated in what we have observed of his intent in dining with publicans and sinners: [11] namely, that he was the Servant to be identified with transgressors (Isa. 53:12) and that in him salvation is extended to the Gentiles. Accomplishment of the Servant's mission, which included the Gentiles' salvation, had been reserved for the

[11] *Supra,* p. 40.

end-time. In according table fellowship to the ungodly and claiming authority to forgive their sins, Jesus said in effect that that time is now present and that Israel's once narrow bounds have been split wide open. When he initiated a meal as the guest of Zacchaeus, a hated tax collector, the Jews murmured, but the word would not be muffled: "Today salvation has come to this house, since he also is a son of Abraham" (Luke 19:9). So the feast on the mountain, God's feast for all peoples (Isa. 25:6), has already begun!

The arrival of the Messianic age is dramatized even more sharply in the feeding miracles attributed to Jesus. Luke (ch. 9:10-17) and John (ch. 6:1-13) record one: the feeding of the five thousand, reported also in Matt. 14:13-21 and Mark 6:32-44. Matthew (ch. 15:32-38) and Mark (ch. 8:1-9) record an additional feeding of four thousand people. It used to be widely held that the accounts of two feedings are based on variant traditions of the same incident, but scholarship is now less inclined to dogmatism about this. Whether one or two feedings occurred, however, the major thrust was that of Messianic feasting, denoting a realized eschatology.[12]

Each account, Luke's especially (ch. 9:11), is in a context of healing — and healing was to be one of the Messiah's great works. Also, Jesus is seen providing in a humanly impossible situation, with an abundance of food remaining — a note often struck in Old Testament descriptions of Israel's feasting in the days of her final salvation.[13] Not to be overlooked either are the baskets of food reported to have been collected: twelve, suggesting establishment of the new Israel; and seven,

---

[12] The miracle-feeding traditions likely came under eucharistic influences, especially since the discourse of John 6:53-56, probably a later addition itself, has a clearly eucharistic tone. But it is unthinkable that either Jesus or his reporters regarded the feedings themselves as eucharistic. They would not suppose those unbelieving, murmuring Jews (vs. 25 ff.) were participating either actually *or* symbolically in a sacrament that requires repentance and faith to be valid. The feedings themselves were solely a compassionate proclamation of the Messianic age.
[13] Amos 9:13; Isa. 49:9-10; 51:14; 55:1-2; Ezek. 47:9-12; Zech. 8:12; Joel 2:24-26; 3:18.

the holy number, signifying completion or fullness. But most striking is Mark's clear allusion to the Davidic shepherd of Ezek., ch. 34 — the one God would send to his hungering sheep, who had been allowed by false shepherds to grow thin. Jesus saw the throng, we are told, " and he had compassion on them, because they were like sheep without a shepherd" (Mark 6:34). Then he taught them, and then he fed them: David has come!

Indicating a futurist eschatology. In regard to Jesus' use of the figure of feasting to express a futurist eschatology, we find a clue in one of his table encounters with the Pharisees. Hearing him mention the resurrection of believers, someone was moved to comment, " Blessed is he who shall eat bread in the kingdom of God!" (Luke 14:15). Whereupon Jesus, surrounded by men who would confine redemption to the Jews, hastened to say in effect that such feasting *will* be held, even though initial invitations have been refused (by the Jews), for invitations to attend will be accepted by others (Gentiles).

That this Lucan reference looks to the final consummation in the Kingdom is confirmed by a similar word in Matt. 8:11-12, where the feasting again relates to the Gentiles' salvation, only this time explicitly in context of the Last Judgment:

I tell you, many will come from east and west and sit at table with Abraham, Isaac, and Jacob in the kingdom of heaven, while the sons of the kingdom will be thrown into the outer darkness; there men will weep and gnash their teeth.

So the tension in New Testament eschatology between " the Kingdom at hand " and " the Kingdom to come " was expressed under the figure of Messianic feasting even prior to the Last Supper. The way had been well prepared for Jesus Messiah to meet at table with his disciples in the upper room, where he would offer them, by means of a meal, the gift of eschatological salvation then and there; and where, at the same time, he would point them to another, future feasting — a feasting that would mean utter salvation for them.

THE LAST SUPPER AND MESSIANIC FEASTING

Turning now toward the eschatological character of eucharistic worship itself, we recall once again that the Lord's Supper was understood to have essentially the same meaning as the Last Supper. And the fact to note is this: the Synoptic accounts of the meal in the upper room show it to be present Messianic feasting and indication of the feasting to come.

As present Messianic feasting. The present tense or realized aspect of Messianic, eschatological feasting at the Last Supper is immediately evident in the setting. The table fellowship is that of the Messiah and his new community. Originally twelve in number, the disciples have been called as the elders and representatives of new Israel. They are of Jewish *and* Gentile stock. Already many have come from east and west and sit at table with Abraham, Isaac, and Jacob!

This eschatological setting of the Supper is also implied in its paschal character. Though nothing in early Passover ritual commanded a forward-looking hope, the meal had assumed an increasingly eschatological outlook, fostered by its historical emphasis. A regard for the past, viewing God's mercy and power as revealed in the exodus, prompted a regard for the future: he who had released his people from Egypt's unshakable bonds would not forget or forsake them. Thus the Passover fitly served as an expression of hope for a new deliverance. Hence the formula used in later observance: " This year, here, next year in the land of Israel; this year slaves, next year free men all." Moreover, by Jesus' day the appearance of the Messiah himself was linked with the Passover. Therefore, in the Johannine account of the feeding of the five thousand, a sign of the Messianic age, the Passover, is intrusively mentioned (John 6:4). And there existed a contemporary hope that Messiah would come to his people on Passover night: " On this night they were saved, and on this night they will be saved " (Mekh. Exod. 12:42). Was it only coincidence that

Jesus' last meal with his disciples, according to Synoptic tradition, fell on that precise night? Or did he not make it the particular night to dish out the end-time salvation to them? [14]

Not only the setting but also the service witnesses to the Last Supper as present Messianic feasting. As we have seen, the common element in the Old Testament's three references to specifically Messianic feasting is the Messiah's humility. And in the upper room, Jesus is the Servant par excellence: the Messiah whose single concern is to minister to his people's needs, even at the cost of his own dignity and comfort. Prefiguring what the cross will mean for him, he washes the disciples' feet in abject self-humiliation (John 13:1 ff.). Did he not tell Zebedee's sons, when they selfishly requested seats of honor in the Kingdom, that his table manners are those of One who came not to be served but to serve (Mark 10:45; cf. Luke 22:27)? Such are his manners here! He is the humble Servant Messiah who, in view of his being broken in obedience to the point of outpoured blood, serves up salvation for others to take. And that, we have discovered, was the primary meaning of Messianic feasting — to receive God's salvation in dependence on him.

The upshot of all this is that the Last Supper, and consequently the Lord's Supper, do not merely anticipate some future eschatological feasting. Each is itself the future feasting, the " realized " Messianic feasting of God's new age.

As indication of the feasting to come. The Last Supper does indicate nonetheless that there is still a feasting to come. As the Passover itself looked backward and forward, Jesus' eucharistic words direct faith both to what has happened — what is presently ours in his obedience unto death — and to its grand consummation.

The so-called vow of abstinence is the pointed word here:

---

[14] This is even more striking from the position adopted herein that Jesus, in making the meal a Passover, either privately anticipated the official calendar or followed some other calendar; see Appendix D.

Truly, I say to you, I shall not drink again of the fruit of the vine until that day when I drink it new in the kingdom of God. (Mark 14:25; cf. esp. Luke 22:16, 18, referring to the Passover.)

In other words: " This is not all. It is Messianic feasting, but there is more ahead. There is yet the day when this Passover, which now takes on new meaning in me, will be perfectly fulfilled; the day when this new exodus deliverance will be fully realized in every aspect of my people's life."

Joachim Jeremias has persuasively argued that the phrase *ou mē* in the vow not only expressed Jesus' determination to suffer in unreserved dedication of his life to the Father; it also was a prayerlike oath to assure the disciples, during subsequent trials, of the certainty of the end.[15] In any event, the futurist reference is unquestionable. The disciples, to whom salvation has come as a present reality, were to keep face forward, looking to the day when the meaning of the paschal meal would be complete in the Kingdom of God. And that, we know, is exactly what they did.

Now, something of this is implied in what we have learned about the meaning of Messianic feasting itself. Such feasting, representing the reception of salvation in the end-time, signified that the future life of the redeemed would be lived in favorable fellowship with God and in utter dependence upon him. It was to be, therefore, not a single meal that Israel would eat once and then take leave of for other things. Rather, it was to be a continual feasting, an " eternal " feasting; for life is necessarily subject to God, who is Giver and Sustainer of life. So, in the sense of what Messianic feasting *means*,[16] we are to understand that the feasting will necessarily continue — yes, in heaven too, lest we suppose that life in that realm could

[15] Joachim Jeremias, *The Eucharistic Words of Jesus*, tr. by Arnold Ehrhardt (The Macmillan Company, 1955), pp. 165–172.
[16] Note the italics. I am concerned only with the *meaning* of Messianic feasting and do not imply that physical food itself will be necessary for life in the Kingdom, as if the resurrection body will be subject to the control of natural, biological laws as we know them.

somehow operate independently of God. The end is on its way, to be sure, but there will always be Messianic feasting!

The Church's Eucharistic Affirmation

This, then, we affirm when celebrating the Lord's, the Messiah's, Supper: the Kingdom has come and is still to come. End-time salvation is ours right now, yet we long for the day when it will be perfected for all the elect. God has wrought it, and he who has begun a good work in us will bring it to sure completion. That, and more, we say about him.

But when gathered at the Messiah's Table, we make an affirmation about ourselves as well. On the one hand, we dare to claim that in Christ we are God's righteous, new-covenant people. How else could we possibly enjoy communion with him? Indeed, how could we participate in Messianic feasting at all, save as men who share Jesus' obedience? Of course, in and by ourselves we are *not* obedient. It is necessary to keep that in mind. But we are not summoned to approach the Table in terror, nor to depart from it in remorse. Just as feeding at the Messiah's hands prophetically meant to be established under his rule, we who feast at Jesus' Table do so on no merits of our own. Rather, we congregate as ones who are constituted righteous in him.

On the other hand, we affirm that we are a dependent people, now and forever. The gift offered to us by way of the bread and wine, the gift of salvation, is what we always have needed and always will need. Messianic feasting is not for us, any more than it was for the prophets, something to do and be done with. Instead, in the sense of what it means, it is the thing we have to do as long as there is any redeemed life for us. This dependency on God we gladly acknowledge. Did we sit at the Table only last week or last month? Perhaps. But we will sit there next time, and then again, to confess our need and give thanks that God in Christ is meeting it. And we will look with joy to the feasting in the Kingdom to come, when this confession and this thanksgiving will get the pure and perfect expression which at the moment we would but cannot give.

APPENDIX

A. THE TEXT OF LUKE

The longer versus the shorter text of Luke, ch. 22, is the only textual problem of real importance in the accounts of the eucharistic words. It involves a number of variant readings primarily originating in the omission of vs. 19b-20. The position favoring the longer text (vs. 17-20) is decisively argued by Joachim Jeremias,[1] to whom I am obviously in debt.

External evidence one-sidedly supports the longer text. Only the Greek Manuscript D, a few Old Latin versions, and the Old Syriac read the shorter. Also, whereas all forms of the latter may be explained as derived from the West,[2] the longer text was found not only in the East, where it originated, but in the West as well. Marcion read v. 20, indicating knowledge of the longer text; and possibly even Tatian witnesses to it.

Those preferring the shorter reading [3] consistently cite two internal facts: (1) the longer is non-Lucan in character; and (2) the shorter is by far the more difficult reading. The first, however, is to be expected, in that vs. 19b-20 issue from a

[1] Joachim Jeremias, *The Eucharistic Words of Jesus*, tr. by Arnold Ehrhardt (The Macmillan Company, 1955), pp. 87–106; see p. 106n1, for others agreeing. About the same case, in less detail, is made by A. J. B. Higgins, *The Lord's Supper in the New Testament* (Alec R. Allenson, Inc., 1952), pp. 37–43.

[2] Jeremias, *op. cit.*, pp. 89–91.

[3] *Ibid.*, p. 100n1, gives an extensive list.

liturgical formula and thus naturally are non-Lucan in style. As for the second fact, the shorter text is simply too difficult, even though the rules of textual criticism generally favor shorter and more difficult readings. It presupposes a cup-bread sequence in eucharistic practice that cannot be found anywhere else.[4] If, to skirt this difficulty, one suggests that the shorter and presumably original text was a *disciplina arcani*, designed to keep the Sacrament a secret and thus protected from public abuse, a theory of *disciplina arcani* works just as well to account for the shortening of the longer text, assuming it was the original.

But the greatest trouble with the shorter reading is its utter inability to explain the geographical distribution of the variants. It was apparently found only in the West; but if it was the original text, it of course originated in the East — yet left no trace there! Surely " It is not reasonable to suppose that the original text was preserved in a pure form only in the West and was wholly obliterated in the East, from which it came." [5] Conversely, the longer text originated in the East, was kept intact there, and made its way into the West as well. Though the reason for its being subsequently shortened remains conjectural, its distribution easily accounts for the shorter text's appearance. To prefer the latter, then, is to get unnecessarily tangled with gross improbabilities and to discount the evidence as a whole.

B. THE REMEMBRANCE SAYING

Since it is found only in I Cor. 11:24-25 (twice) and Luke 22:19b, and since Mark's formulation of the bread and wine sayings seems to represent the earliest text underlying the New Testament accounts of the eucharistic words, one might conclude that the reference to remembrance was a later addition to Jesus' words.

[4] Didache 9 notwithstanding; see Higgins, *op. cit.*, pp. 38–39.
[5] Frederic G. Kenyon, *The Text of the Greek Bible*, new ed. (London: Gerald Duckworth & Co., Ltd., 1949), p. 220.

But the question of authenticity here is not simply " early " Mark versus "late" Paul. There is evidence that the Pauline tradition is itself early and that Luke's account, rather than depending directly on the Marcan and Pauline traditions, possibly represents yet a third variation of the earliest liturgical formula.[1] Mark's omission of the reference may therefore be against not one but two early and independent traditions that include it.

Moreover, it is noteworthy that *eis anamnēsin* reflects early Palestinian usage.[2] Also, since Mark's account implies liturgical usage, we suppose it was not intended to report everything Jesus said when distributing the elements. Further still, Paul claimed to have passed on to the Corinthians what he had received through tradition,[3] presumably from members of the Jerusalem church, some of whom attended the Last Supper; and it is questionable that he, who had troubles enough with the Judaizers in that church, would have opened himself to their attack by attributing to Jesus certain words that could not be substantiated as authentic.

Why was the reference omitted in the Marcan tradition? Gregory Dix, following Paul's account of two references to remembrance, suggests the double reference initially served to bring the bread and wine sayings together and was later omitted when the rite was firmly established.[4] Since these sayings were originally separated by the meal proper, Jesus used the remembrance motif to connect them in a new meaning, to the exclusion of all that came between. Later, when they existed side by side in eucharistic practice, this original function was no longer needed; so the reference was dropped.

Though ingenious, Dom Dix's explanation stresses too much a purely functional significance of the reference and not at all its interpretative significance. It may have incidentally served

[1] Cf. Jeremias, *op. cit.*, pp. 102–103; Higgins, *op. cit.*, pp. 40–44.
[2] Jeremias, *op. cit.*, p. 161.
[3] *Infra*, p. 114.
[4] Gregory Dix, *The Shape of the Liturgy,* 2d ed. (London: The Dacre Press, 1945), pp. 67–69.

such a purpose; certainly the bread and wine sayings *were* brought together. But, evidently, Paul and others considered the original intent of the reference to be relevant even after the rite was fixed. Why, then, was it omitted in the Marcan tradition? Probably because its particular meaning was itself assumed in the church's practice. Whatever eating and drinking " unto the remembrance of Jesus " meant must have soon been taken for granted in eucharistic worship. That this was actually the case is indicated above: the remembrance motif in Paul's and Luke's accounts does not alter or extend the sacramental meaning of Jesus' words as Mark reports them, but only makes it more emphatic.[5]

C. JESUS' INSTITUTION OF THE LORD'S SUPPER

The traditional view that Jesus " instituted " the Lord's Supper has been disclaimed by critics who substitute an origin in Hellenism's mystery religions. From obvious similarities, it is suggested that the New Testament sacramental teaching betrays a Hellenistic influence that took hold via Paul. At first the Eucharist bore no sacramental import, but the apostle to the Gentiles, who would be " all things to all men " and who was himself influenced by the pagan mysteries, gave it a new meaning which he believed he got by direct revelation.

The most articulate argument for this general position is by Hans Lietzmann,[1] who saw New Testament evidence of two types of early eucharistic practice: a Jerusalem type and a Pauline type.[2] The former, rooted in the " breaking of bread " meals mentioned in Acts, which allegedly had no special rela-

---

[5] *Supra*, p. 82.

[1] Hans Lietzmann, *Mass and Lord's Supper*, tr. by Dorothea H. G. Reeve (Leiden: E. J. Brill, Publisher, 1953–1958), pp. 195–208.

[2] See Higgins, *op. cit.*, p. 58n1, for others reaching similar conclusions. Oscar Cullmann's modification of Lietzmann's position is now in English translation: " The Meaning of the Lord's Supper in Primitive Christianity," *Essays on the Lord's Supper,* by Oscar Cullmann and F. J. Leenhardt (John Knox Press, 1958), pp. 5–23.

tion to the Last Supper and lacked reference to Christ's death, was an eschatological joy feast, dwelling on his presence and looking to Parousia. The latter depended finally on Paul, who refashioned an existing sacramental Eucharist, itself evidenced in Mark and based in pagan memorial feasts (called "remembrances"). He connected this so-called Hellenistic Eucharist with the Last Supper and made it a memorial of Christ's death. Only after this Pauline transformation did the Hellenistic Eucharist affect the church's practice.[3]

Besides the similarities, four specific witnesses have generally been called to support the mystery-religions theory: (1) the references in Acts 2:42, 46 to "the breaking of bread," taken to imply a wineless Eucharist; (2) the shorter text of Luke 22:17-19a, which omits the remembrance motif and the wine saying about Jesus' blood; (3) Didache 9, which also might indicate a Eucharist with no reference to Christ's death; and (4) Paul's statement that he received his teaching "from the Lord" (I Cor. 11:23), supposedly implying direct, special revelation and thus accounting for his alleged eucharistic innovations.

Similarities with Hellenistic sacramentalism must be weighed cautiously, since it is an axiom in the study of origins that parallelism by itself implies neither dependence nor necessary influence. Further, the above four witnesses said to support the theory may be turned against it. (1) If the term in Acts 2:42, 46 refers to a Eucharist, so must it also in ch. 20:7 regarding Paul's stay in Troas. But it is not likely that Paul, who stressed the wine's significance in terms of the new covenant in Jesus' blood, would have engaged in a wineless Eucharist; nor is it likely that the same term should be used in Acts to denote essentially different kinds of practice. (2) The shorter text of Luke is decidedly the inferior reading, as noted above in Appendix A. Besides, to base a theory of eucharistic origins in Luke at all, setting Luke in historical preference to

[3] For criticism of Lietzmann's formulation, cf. Higgins, *op. cit.*, pp. 61 ff.; Cullmann, *op. cit., passim.*

the earlier traditions of Mark and I Corinthians, is strictly poor procedure. (3) The reference of Didache 9 is most probably to the agape which preceded the Eucharist, not to the Eucharist itself.[4] And (4) the phrase " from the Lord," particularly as it is used with *paralabein* (to receive tradition) and *paradidonai* (to deliver tradition), is generally regarded to be a claim for tradition, not for direct and special revelation [5] — a conclusion enforced by Paul's usage elsewhere of *paralabein* especially.[6]

But the most farfetched aspect of the mystery-religions theory is the supposition that paganism could infiltrate the church's worship and in so short a time utterly pervert the original Eucharist, with the perversion assigned to Jesus himself. In which case Paul, or whoever was responsible for the hoax, had to get the church's agreement on it, even though some who had attended the Last Supper presumably knew better!

The mystery-religions theory is therefore suspect and need not stand in the way of our reaffirming Jesus' institution of the Sacrament. Moreover, as the present study shows, New Testament eucharistic teaching can be explained as deriving from Hebraic sacramentalism; a Hellenistic origin is neither required nor finally even relevant. Further, the New Testament accounts of the eucharistic words imply liturgical usage. That Mark, whose account represents possibly the oldest liturgical form,[7] was free to use such a formula in reporting what occurred in the upper room — this indicates what extremely early celebrants assumed: namely, that the Last Supper and the Lord's Supper bear essentially the same sacramental import.

[4] Jeremias, *op. cit.*, pp. 84–85.

[5] But cf. Oscar Cullmann's suggestion that the phrase may signify a direct revelation *through* the tradition, in which tradition the Lord is active: "'KYRIOS' as Designation for the Oral Tradition concerning Jesus (*Paradosis* and *Kyrios*)," *Scottish Journal of Theology*, 3:180–197 (June, 1950).

[6] Cf. I Cor. 15:1, 3; Gal. 1:9; Phil. 4:9; I Thess. 2:13; 4:1; II Thess. 3:6.

[7] See Jeremias, *op. cit.*, pp. 106–132.

D. THE CHARACTER AND DATE OF THE LAST SUPPER

Was the Last Supper a Passover? When was it held? The problem is complicated by the fact that the Synoptics and John both yield evidence indicating a Passover and yet opposing a date of Nisan 15, the date for Passover observance.

Mark (ch. 14:12, 14, 16), followed by Matthew, and Luke (ch. 22:8, 11, 13, 15) identify the meal as a Passover. In support of this Joachim Jeremias has accumulated a mass of incidental data,[1] the most important of which follows: (1) rather than in Bethany, to which Jesus regularly went in the evenings of his last stay in Jerusalem, the meal was eaten in the overcrowded city where the Passover had to be eaten; (2) it began in the evening and lasted into the night, as did the Passover; (3) Jesus and the disciples reclined, which was Passover custom at the time; (4) a dish preceded the breaking of the bread, mostly in Passover observance; (5) the closing hymn suggests the second half of the Passover *Hallel;* and (6) rather than returning to Bethany after the meal, Jesus and the disciples went to the Mount of Olives, keeping with a Passover ruling that the night be spent in the district of Jerusalem, which was enlarged for Passover and included Gethsemane but not Bethany. Since nothing in the description of the meal itself necessarily negates a paschal interpretation,[2] the only adequate explanation for this incidental evidence – in the Synoptics *and* John [3] – is that the Supper, named a Passover, was a Passover in fact.

But there are conflicting time references. According to Mark 14:12 (cf. Matt. 26:17) and Luke 22:7, the meal occurred on Nisan 15, whereas John 18:28 clearly dates the cruci-

---

[1] Jeremias, *op. cit.*, pp. 14–37.
[2] *Ibid.*, pp. 37–46.
[3] The evidence under (1), (2), (3), and (6) is found in both, that under (4) and (5) in the Synoptics alone.

fixion Nisan 14.[4] Also, as noted below, the Synoptic accounts themselves hold incidental difficulties for a date of Nisan 15.

A major way to " solve " the problem has been to side with either the Synoptic or Johannine chronology and coordinately to conclude the meal was or was not a Passover.[5] The most popular explanation of those so favoring the Johannine dating — i.e., the Supper was a so-called kiddush meal [6] — is representative of the failing of this position in general. Besides making the kiddush antedate by twenty-four hours that which it sanctifies (see the note just cited), it cannot fully account for the cumulative incidental evidence indicating Passover regulations and observance.

Of those favoring the Synoptic chronology and teaching, Dr. Jeremias is champion. His answers to the objections against a date of Nisan 15 are labored at points, but he has considered every significant objection and has made the best defense yet for this position. The chink in his armor, however, is his less-than-satisfying explanation of the Sanhedrin's meeting and condemnation of Jesus on Nisan 15, which Jewish law forbade.[7] Citing the opinion of Rabbi Akibah, he claims Jesus' case was a legal exception to the law of no judging on feast days, and concludes that he had to be tried and executed at once. But it is not certain that the ruling of legal exception applied in Jesus' day. Rabbi Akibah's opinion was later contra-

---

[4] John 13:1, 29b; 19:14, 31 are also often cited for Nisan 14; but Jeremias, *op. cit.*, pp. 54–56, discounts them, even seeing in John 13:29b a trace of the Synoptic dating.

[5] *Ibid.*, pp. 177–183, giving an extensive bibliography for and against a Passover.

[6] A regular Friday afternoon meal that was ended or interrupted by a kiddush, a prayer of sanctification said over a cup of wine at the beginning of the Sabbath or a feast day. It is suggested that, since Jesus and the disciples were to be at the Temple on Friday for the slaying of the Passover lambs, the meal was put back to Thursday.

[7] Jeremias, *op. cit.*, pp. 49–53. His suggestion that the objection, if valid, weighs equally against the Johannine chronology (since capital crimes could not be tried on the *eve* of a Sabbath or feast day either; cf. Sanh. 4:1; b. Sanh. 35a) holds only if the Sanhedrin tried Jesus legally; but, as noted below, this cannot be proved.

dicted by R. Judah ben El 'ai (Tos Sanh. 11:7; b. Sanh. 89a); and as one of the best authorities observes, it generally holds that R. Judah, when opposing R. Akibah, "harks back to the Mishna of the older Tannaim." [8] Further, the ruling of legal exception, requiring trial and execution "before all the people" (hence on Nisan 15, while the city was still full), seems to justify the Sanhedrin's meeting only if it was literally a trial, issuing in a legal sentence. Yet conclusive proof is wanting that it was more than a preliminary inquiry with a view to making recommendations to the Roman procurator, who would pass legal judgment himself.[9] The Jews admitted *they* could not put a man to death (John 18:31); and it is a matter of unanimous record that they anxiously waited for Pilate to issue an effective sentence. So the Sanhedrin's meeting continues as a difficulty for a date of Nisan 15 and, alongside certain other objections also requiring labored answers, impugns the Synoptic chronology.

This, then, is the situation: the Last Supper was apparently a Passover, but the Johannine date of Nisan 14 for the crucifixion best accords with certain events of Passion Week. If the conflicting chronologies are not to be reconciled, I must conclude that Jesus privately "anticipated" the Passover, celebrating it early (without a lamb). That "such a private anticipation of the Passover ceremony would constitute a serious breach of the Mosaic law" [10] is a puny objection regarding One who considered himself fit to reinterpret the law. Surely *he* would have thought himself free to celebrate the Passover early and thereby give it new meaning in view of his own full sacrifice!

Beyond this point discussions are even more conjectural. However, two suggestions, forms of what may be called the

---

[8] Hermann L. Strack, *Introduction to the Talmud and Midrash* (Jewish Publication Society of America, 1931), p. 23.
[9] Cf. Joseph Klausner, *Jesus of Nazareth*, tr. by Herbert Danby (The Macmillan Company, 1925), pp. 102, 333 ff.
[10] Jeremias, *op. cit.*, p. 7n2.

two-Passovers theory, deserve mention.[11] One is based on the difference between the Sadducean and Pharisaic interpretations of Lev. 23:11, 15. Whereas the Sadducees reckoned therefrom that Pentecost and Passover always had to fall on the eve of a weekly Sabbath (as in the year of Jesus' death, according to John), the Pharisees judged that the day for observance depended solely on the first sighting of the new moon. Supposing that this difference was an issue the year Jesus died, it has been suggested (1) that the Pharisees and Jesus observed Passover (with or without a lamb) on Thursday evening, which the Synoptic dating follows; and (2) that the Sadducees observed it twenty-four hours later, which the Johannine dating follows. Since the Sadducees controlled the Temple at the time, the Johannine dating of Nisan 14 represents the official calendar. The conflicting chronologies are thus reconciled, and the internal difficulties vanish. It is then understandable how *both* the Synoptic and Johannine traditions could attest to the paschal character of the Supper and to the Sanhedrin's meeting, yet without either tradition thereby partially refuting its own time reference.

The other suggestion, coming primarily from Mlle Annie Jaubert and winning notable support,[12] is that Jesus and the disciples ate the Passover on Tuesday evening of Passion Week, in accordance with the fixed dating of a solar calendar evident in ancient Israel and extant at the time. From evidence of Qumran Cave 4 it is now clear that the Qumran sectarians followed the same calendaric system as the book of Jubilees, fixing Nisan 15 always on Tuesday. Although the Jubilees calendar may never have been official in ancient

---

[11] For yet another attempt at harmonization, suggesting the Synoptics follow a fixed calendar of Diaspora Judaism, see Massey H. Shepherd, Jr., "Are Both the Synoptics and John Correct about the Date of Jesus' Death?" *Journal of Biblical Literature*, 80:123–132 (June, 1961).

[12] Annie Jaubert, *La Date de la cène: Calendrier biblique et liturgie chrétienne* (Paris: J. Gabalda, 1957). For reactions pro and con, cf. the works noted *ibid.*, p. 123n1, especially the favorable review of Skehan for more detailed presentation of Jaubert's thesis.

Israel, its prototype may be found there; and there is reason to believe that a solar calendar continued to be used for religious practices by "peripheral" Jews — e.g., the Galileans — who were outside the immediate influence of Jerusalem, where the official calendar was lunar. Moreover, Matthew Black calls attention to (1) telescoping tendencies in Mark, especially with regard to Passion Week; (2) evidence that Luke reflects an independent tradition indicating a longer period between Jesus' arrest and crucifixion than is indicated in Mark's "telescopic" account; and (3) traces in John of a tradition placing the Last Supper and arrest earlier than Thursday evening and night.[13] One may therefore believe that the Synoptic dating follows a solar calendar, whereas the Johannine dating represents the official, lunar calendar.

Although it is probably too early for a dogmatic evaluation of this view, there is much to commend it, not the least of which is its explanation of the conflicting New Testament chronologies with but a minimum of difficulties of its own. Yet its greatest merit is allowing more time for the many events said to have occurred (without apparent rush!) between Jesus' arrest and crucifixion, events which otherwise must be crammed into an inexplicably short period:

Notice the list: Jesus is brought before the high priest; the chief priests, the elders and the scribes are all assembled (Mark 14.53), as is the whole Sanhedrin (Mark 14.55); witnesses are sought and cannot be found (Mark 14.55); the evidence was considerable but it did not cohere (Mark 14.56); later witnesses accuse him of wishing to destroy the temple (Mark 14.56-58); then comes the judgement of the high priest. Is it really likely that all this took place in a single night?[14]

[13] Matthew Black, "The Arrest and Trial of Jesus and the Date of the Last Supper," *New Testament Essays: Studies in Memory of Thomas Walter Manson*, ed. by A. J. B. Higgins (Manchester: Manchester University Press, 1959), pp. 19–33.
[14] A. Gilmore, "The Date and Significance of the Last Supper," *Scottish Journal of Theology*, 14:264–265 (Sept., 1961).

INDEX OF SCRIPTURE REFERENCES